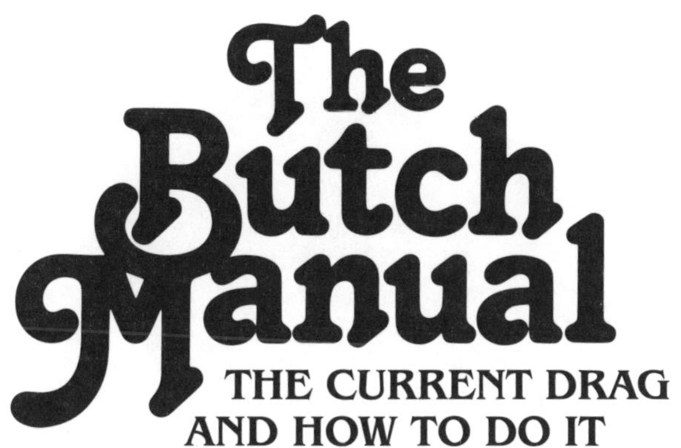

The Butch Manual

THE CURRENT DRAG AND HOW TO DO IT

By Clark Henley

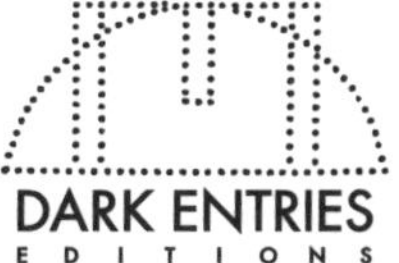
DARK ENTRIES EDITIONS

First Edition 2025

LIBRARY OF CONGRESS CATALOGING IN PUBLICATION DATA
Henley, Clark.
The butch manual.
Reprint. Originally published: New York : Seahorse Press, 1982.
Sex Customs–Anecdotes, facetiae, satire, etc.
Sexual Deviation–Anecdotes, facetiae, satire, etc.

ISBN 979-8-9851704-0-5

Designed by Julian Hamer
Cover Design & Art Direction by David Martin & Felice Picano
Cover Photos by Rod Mitchel
Body Photos by Clark Henley, Sam Hale & Rod Mitchel
Layout Reproduction by Eloise Shir-Juen Leigh
Photo Retouching by Mark Hanson
Edited by Josh Cheon

Body text has been set in 10 point Times New Roman;
headings in 10 point and 14 point Beguiat Pro ITC.

Printed in Canada
Printed by The Prolific Group

DARK ENTRIES EDITIONS
910 Larkin Street, San Francisco, CA 94109
www.darkentriesrecords.com

For John

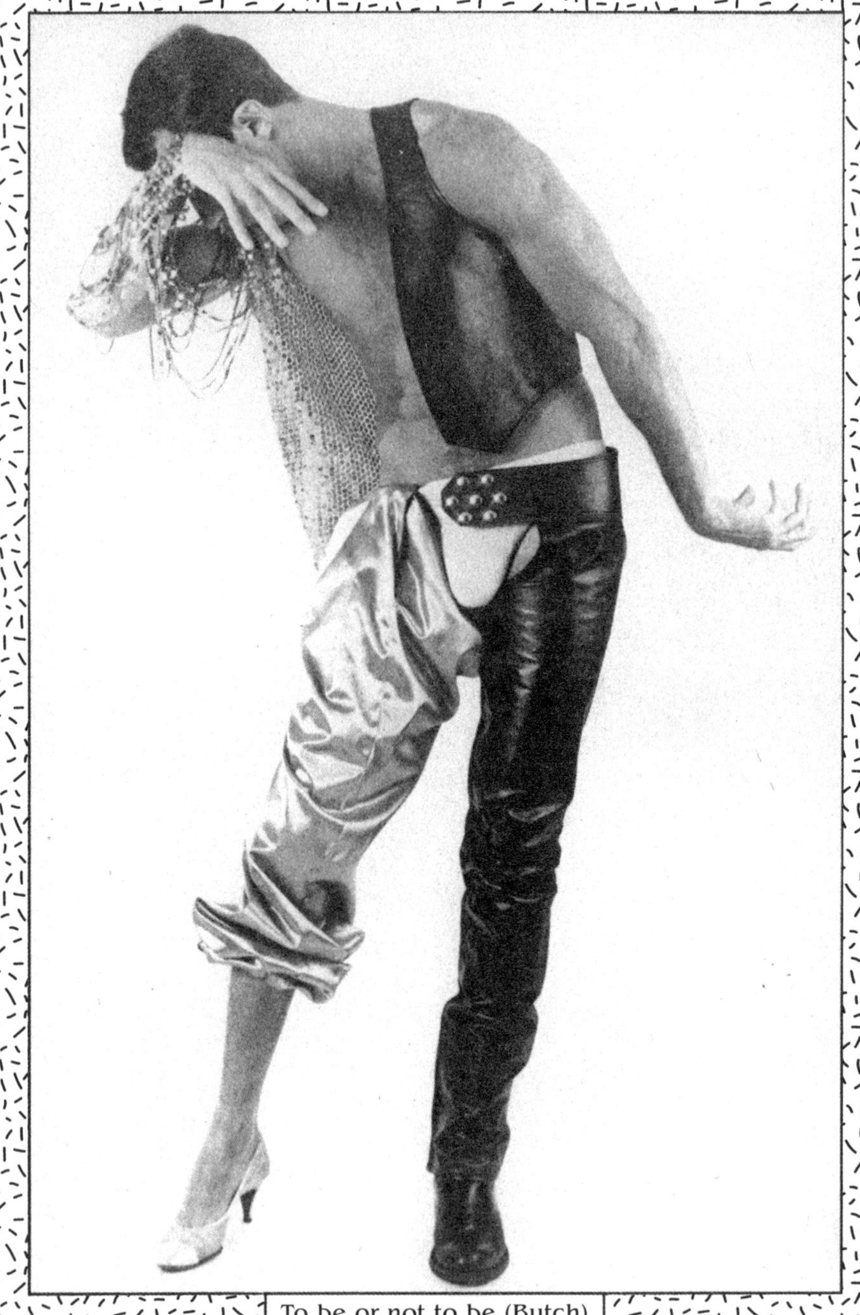

To be or not to be (Butch)

Foreword

by Brendan McHugh

Are books about masculinity lacking in laughs? Do you snicker at "masc for masc"... yet secretly strive to pass? Or, are you feeling driven to claim the Dad within? Perhaps you're tempted to try, just ever so, to "butch it up"? Well, fortunately, Clark Henley wrote *the book for you*. Here it is, back in print after decades: *The Butch Manual: The New Drag and How to Do It!* No longer will you have to scour eBay, take out Klarna payment plans, or commit hundreds of dollars for a first edition copy. *Butch* is back and taking no prisoners! Now you, too, can learn how to walk, eat, party, drug, sleep, and talk (if you must), just like the genuine Butch article. A new generation of Butches is waiting to be born, and Clark is here to butch-ly push you toward aloof ruggedness. Read on, Mary (a most un-butch way to hail the reader).

The Butch Manual flexed its way into gay and lesbian bookstores in 1982, touting the message that masculinity, specifically butchness, was the latest drag for gay men. Born and raised in San Francisco, Clark moved to Los Angeles in the early 1980s for his writing career. But, he never felt quite like he found his place in the image-conscious town. His inspiration for *Butch* arrived during a family visit to the Kansas City baths. Sitting on a sofa, Clark eavesdropped on two hunky-femmey, farmboys animatedly discussing how to butch it up: keeping the wrist firm, cruising looking uninterested, and correctly crossing one's legs. Clark suspected farmhands and city boys alike could benefit from a campy guide to Butch etiquette. Once back in L.A., the book basically wrote itself. Within a week of sending out his manuscript to gay publishers and writers, Clark made contact with Felice Picano's SeaHorse Press who agreed to take on *Butch*. Excerpts ran in multiple gay magazines with large circulations: *The Advocate, Stallion, Blue Boy,* and *Metra*, to name a few. What made *Butch* buzzy and so easily excerpted was its succinctness. The delicate toeing of satire with sincerity and a whole lot of bite. The book was almost unanimously adored in the thirteen reviews Clark received. Dorothy Allison—a major figure in Lesbian writing and political organizing—loved it. Her experience of reading it in public was one where people's curiosity led them to take the book from her hands, looking to "find" themselves in it, often encountering a line that left them in stitches.

The Butch Manual is a revelation of visual prowess and comical intuitiveness. This reprint of *Butch* revels in the book's biting staying power as it turns focus to a hyper-specific gay white masculinity that queer people still grapple with. The genius in centering Butch as an achievable way of being—while also laughing hysterically at it—is a gift to readers and queer studies scholars alike. To what end will we go as queers to transform ourselves into fantasy? Is fantasy also the path in becoming our true selves? Tragically, Clark's life was cut short in 1988 by AIDS. His last writings on *living* with AIDS were heartfelt but still retained *Butch*'s playful snark, too. Clark's playfulness is deeply needed in a moment where our community is under direct attack. The importance of having an inside joke helps us stay sane as we remain on the political and cultural defense. Thanks to Josh Cheon of Dark Entries, my fellow Butch scholar John Dempsey, the late Felice Picano, and Clark's family, especially Victoria Henley and Carol and Rick Meredith, now you, at last, can hold *Butch* in your hands and start your journey. Prepare to laugh. The great work begins, Stud.

San Francisco, May 2025

Acknowledgments

by Clark Henley

I, myself, know absolutely nothing about being Butch. Luckily, all of my friends consider themselves to be authorities. The writing on the bathroom walls has been read. (One reason some of the following people appear on a first-name basis is because this is a friendly generation; the other reason is because some of these friendly people could lose their jobs if their last names were to appear here. *C'est la guerre.*)

Mack truckloads of thanks to: Edmund White and *States of Desire*, which inspired me to see America first and to overhear the beginning of this book in the Club Baths of Kansas City; all the gay men in Kansas, to be sure; The Laughing Editorial Room: Dan A., James B., Lee Garlington, Stewartness, Stevadore, and the Incredible Sharon McDonald; Larry Paulson for Butch Choreography; Rod Mitchel for Butch Photography; those Adorable Hunks, the Butchest Models on Earth: Budd, David, Greg, Mark, and Taavi (truly a treat to emerge from any Butch Birthday Cake); and a special Butch Bouquet to Joel Leonard's Erector Set, Inc.

More thanks to the Unicorn Icons: John, Dino, and Bette—I mean David, and a special hug to Kris; Rusty (and David), Bonnie, and Group 5; Toutes Les Butches Isadorables; the Gentlemen at Jim Morris Gym; Kit and her Pennies-from-Heaven Co., which allows me to pursue my lavish career as a starving artist; my ex-lover, Peter; his current lover, Don; Don's ex, Larry; Larry's current, John; and John's ex, Whoever that might be; the Incredible Dragon Boy, Sam and his Magnificent Magenta Aura; Joanie B. Loney and Munchkin; and the incomparable Armistead.

Thanks to Robert McQueen; David Goodstein; Norman Laurila and "A Different Light Bookstore"; Joseph M.; John W.; Patty M.; Kim C.; Michael V.; Bill B.; Charlie; my hero, M. S.; the loving B. H.; Steve Schulte, Burke Thompson, Malcolm Boyd, Jim Boyle, and the Gay and Lesbian Community Services Center of Los Angeles; and the tag teams: Courtney and Cynthia, Tory, and Rick and Carol Cafeteria.

Special thanks to Danny Westergard, who has devoted God knows how many brain cells to remembering everything; and to Cathryn, surely an angel; and last, but also the most—to the fabulous Michael Lassell, whose pure gusto lures me out from under my bed, whose immeasurable genius pries my excessive life story from endless split infinitives, and whose generosity to life inspires me to action, reason enough to love him.

Contents

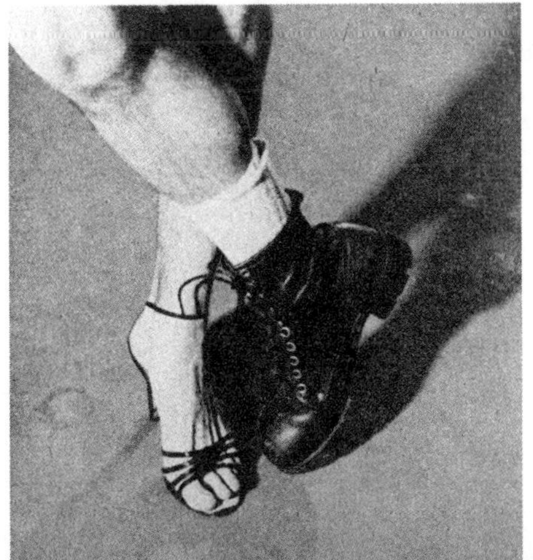

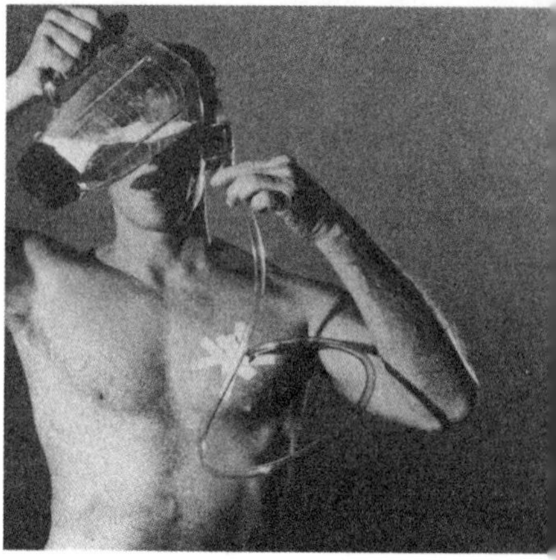

Butch Dressing 51

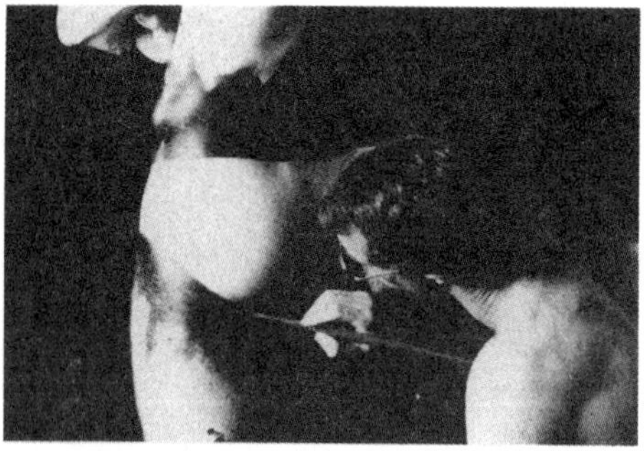

Butch Locale 67

Butch Drugs 77

Butchopoly 85

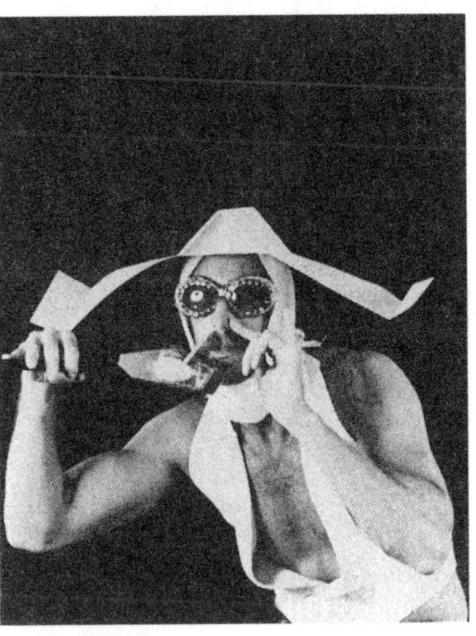

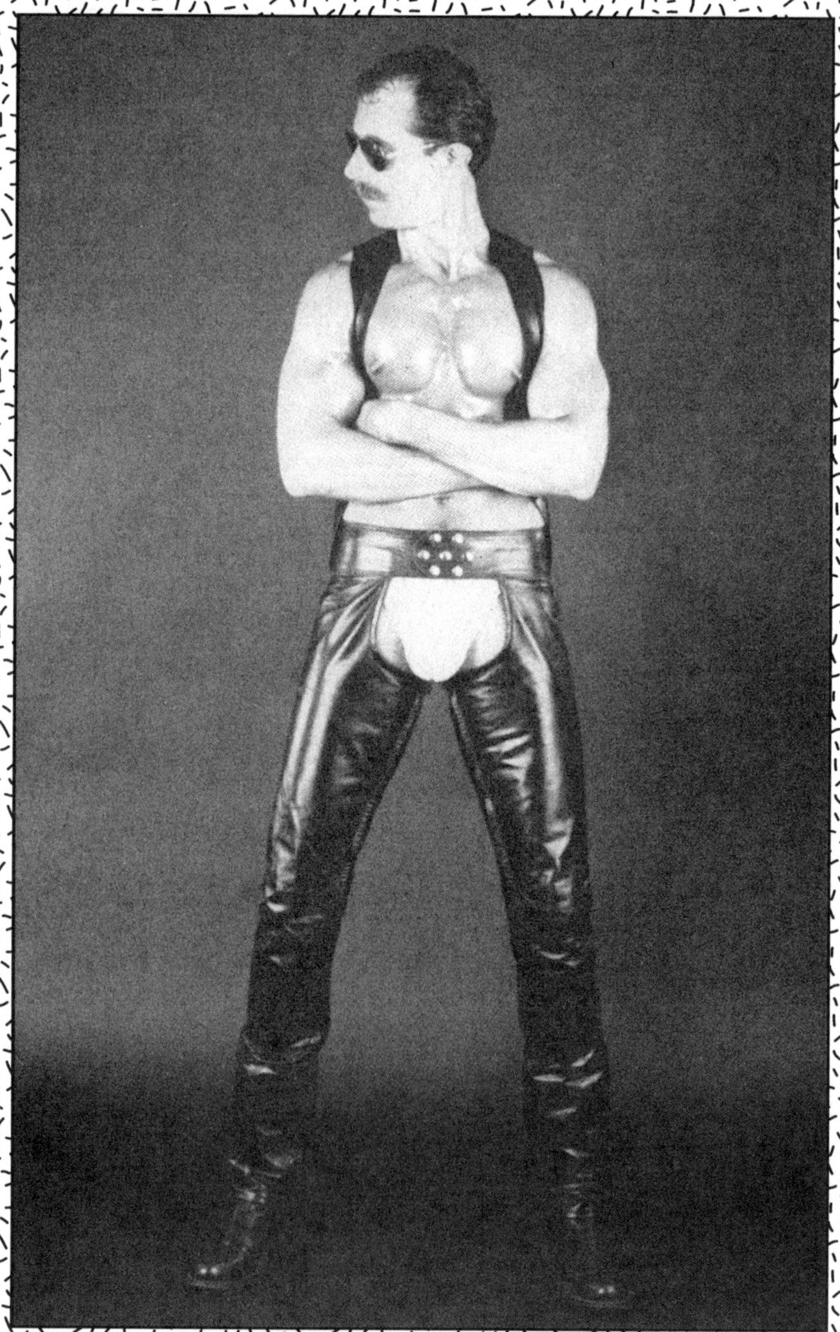

Being Butch

Are you getting laid frequently enough?

Does anyone get laid enough?

Did you feel like you were finally getting somewhere in the self-esteem department? You've stopped trying to deepen your voice when you meet new people. You stopped worrying if you crossed your legs the wrong way. You've finally liberated yourself as a free spirit—only to find that free spirits have gone out of season!

Suddenly the most inconsequential decisions are grounds for a major identity crisis.

—Which color is more fun, party pink or olive drab?

—Which article of clothing is more festive, a feather boa or a constr-uction hat?

—Who would it be more fun to imitate on a New York subway grating—Marilyn Monroe or R2D2?

So why is everyone acting like R2D2?

The answer is simple: because R2D2 is Butch, and Butch is getting laid.

So throw out your heels and get out the construction boots. There's a whole new drag, and it's called Butch.

Relax. No one is born Butch. Most of us are born babies and promptly burst into tears, which is most un-Butch. Yet when some people grow up they become inescapably Butch, while others are still sitting on the side-lines waiting for a miracle. Is it in the genes? Natural selection? Divine intervention?

No. These people have done their homework. They have read the writing on the bathroom walls. They have followed the advice of the graffiti gurus. They've given people what they think the people want. They've gone Butch.

And so can you. Here it is, live, from every toilet in town, *The Butch Manual!*

What is Butch?

BEFORE *(Unbutch)*	**AFTER** *(Butch)*
Furtive glances	Sunglasses
Misquoting Dorothy Parker	Talking dirty
Sexy windblown look (from hairblower)	Sexy windblown look (from motorcycle)
Smiling	Mustaches
Real estate	Large pecs
GQ magazine	Drummer magazine
Perspiration	Sweat
Gold chains	Iron chains
Designer shower curtains	Athlete's foot
Swiss mocha	Taster's Choice
Dizzy	Wasted
Full-length mirror (in bathroom)	Full-length mirror (in bedroom)
Screaming	Yelling
Restraint	Restraints
Camping (on Fire Island)	Camping (on Russian River)
Brie	Velveeta
Cocktails	Cock-sucking
Fainting	Passing out
Romance	Poppers
Cuisinarts	
Betamaxes	
Jacuzzis	
Phone-answering machines	Sex
Automobile alarm systems	
Electric door openers	
Garbage compactors	
Beepers	

The Butch Quiz
(Do You Have Potential?)

In first grade you received a box of crayons. The first crayon you grabbed was:

a. Gray.
b. Navy Blue.
c. Red.
d. Silver.
e. Magenta.

In second grade your favorite thing to do at recess was:

a. Hide in the school's dumpster.
b. Play "crack the whip."
c. Play tether ball.
d. Sneak into the cloak closet and try on everyone else's coats.
e. Hitchhike to the nearest movie theater and see the latest Bergman film.

In third grade you wanted to be in the school's Christmas pageant. The role you coveted was:

a. One of the oxen.
b. Joseph.
c. The Drummer Boy.
d. The Shining Star.
e. God.

During the fourth grade you watched *Leave It to Beaver*. You fantasized that two of the characters were onscreen lovers. Unfortunately, their love scenes were tragically cut from each episode. The two characters in this supposed affair were:

a. Mr. Cleaver and his eldest son, Wally.
b. Wally and his girlfriend (even though she was completely cut out of the script.)
c. Wally and the Beaver.
d. Mrs. Cleaver and Wally's two-faced best friend, Eddie Haskell.
e. Mr. and Mrs. Cleaver.

In the fifth grade each person chose a state to do a report on. You chose:

a. Arkansas.
b. Colorado.
c. Washington, D.C.
d. The Cote d'Azur.
e. Depression.

In the sixth grade, at graduation, the teacher asked everyone what they wanted to be when they grew up. You said:

a. A fireman.
b. A realtor.
c. A husband.
d. A makeup artist.
e. Young.

In seventh grade you suddenly found yourself extremely unpopular. You attributed this to:

a. The scar you got when you fell out the window of the school bus.
b. Your inability to use the guide words in the dictionary.
c. Your braces, your zits, your height, your weight, and seven cowlicks all in front.
d. Throwing like a girl.
e. The fact that your class was mildly retarded, aesthetically if not academically.

In eighth grade, Prom Night finally arrived. You:

a. Took the fattest girl in school and cut up the dance floor.
b. Took the most beautiful girl in school and lost your virginity on the ninth hole of the nearest golf course.
c. Went with the guys and spent the evening getting drunk in the locker room.
d. Went by yourself and asked a girl to dance; when she said no, you went outside and threw up.
e. Decorated the gym within an inch of its life, then stayed home and watched reruns of *Leave It to Beaver*.

When you were sick as a child, your favorite medication was:

a. A bullet to bite on.
b. Two aspirin with a nice cold glass of Coca-Cola.
c. Aspergum.
d. Romilar cough syrup.
e. A very dry vodka martini on the rocks with an olive and two Quaaludes.

The sound most reminiscent of your childhood was:

a. The school lawnmower finding a Coke bottle on the athletic field.
b. The recess bell.
c. Your name being chosen to be on a team for phys ed.
d. Your mother talking on the telephone.
e. The nurse reading your name on the "Excused from phys ed." list.

"Nancy" meant many things while you were growing up. The one and only Nancy for you, however, was:

a. The girl who played with Sluggo.
b. The girl who solved mysteries.
c. The girl who smiled on the arm of her acting politician.
d. The girl who sang "One of these days, these boots are going to walk all over you."
e. The subway stop in Paris.

Disney was your religion as a child. Your most memorable movie moment was when:

a. The alligator ate Captain Hook.
b. Snow White's stepmother was crushed by rocks.
c. Pinocchio turned into a donkey.
d. The mice made Cinderella's dress.
e. Bambi's mother died.

Answers

If you chose lots of *a*'s, you are already extremely Butch. You are also a dyke, no offense intended.

If you chose lots of *b*'s, you are almost as Butch. You are also a heterosexual male, no offense intended.

If you chose lots of *c*'s, this book is what you've been looking for your whole life. Proceed with renewed vigor and memorize every detail.

If you chose lots of *d*'s, you are an accomplished Queen. You could skim this book and have the whole routine down perfectly in fifteen minutes, but you'd give it up immediately because olive-drab bugle beads do not look attractive in a spotlight with a bastard amber gel.

If you chose lots of *e*'s, you are an accomplished Eccentric. This book will not make any sense to you.

The Origins of Butch

After the last dinosaur had dropped dead in the Colorado River Basin, men ventured out of their caves. There were two caves and two different tribes: the Machos and the Fairies. Women were not fond of caves—nor, for that matter, of men—so they spent their time darting about in the bushes.

Civilization was getting off to a rather slow start because there was so little to do. People couldn't very well stand around on bank lines, nor could they go to court to fight unjust parking tickets. They couldn't even dress up in amusing costumes to go on *Let's Make a Deal*! All there was to do, really, was to go down to the riverbank and get tanned.

The Machos marched down to the beach in their Bermuda shorts and drank beer. They dunked one another in the water and then rolled around in the sand until they were dry. They never used oil. (Their first words were, "I don't burn.") They got very burnt and were constantly peeling. They got drunker and clambered around in the bushes brandishing large clubs at the women. (This did not endear them to the women, whose first words were, "Fuck off, you drunken boor.")

The Fairies scampered down to the beach and took off all their clothes. They did a dance to celebrate the sun and anointed one another with lots of lotions, potions, creams, and fragrant oils. (Their first words were, "Honey, you're getting red, let me put on some oil.") After

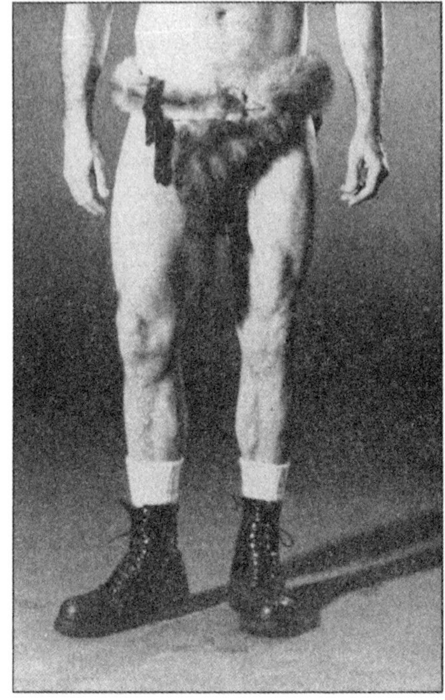

A member of the Macho Tribe

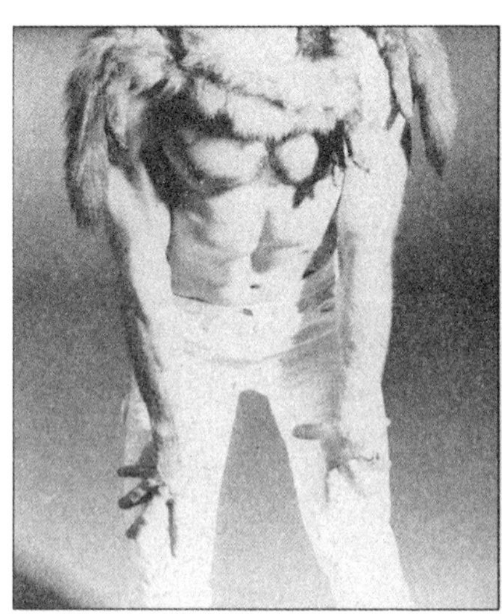

A member of the Fairy Tribe

they swam, they smoked herbs, ate mushrooms, and built sand castles. At night they sat around the campfire and talked about inventing modern dance, hair conditioners, and the word "fabulous." And then they liked to chase one another around in the bushes, rubbing still more oil on each other.

Everything meandered along smoothly until one night when the women hid particularly well and the drunken Machos stumbled around for quite a while bumping into one another. They were in a foul humor by the time they ran into the Fairies, who were giggling and having a splendidly sordid time. The Machos bashed all the Fairies and went home.

To add insult to injury, the Machos showed up at Fairy Beach the next day and kicked sand in all the Fairies' faces. Half of the Fairies stood up and screamed, "Eat shit and die, bitch!" This suggestion did not please the Machos, so they chased the Fairies into the bushes where they've been chasing them ever since, motivation never being the issue.

The other half of the Fairies ran to another part of the bushes and had a meeting.

"Shit, Mary, we gotta hide from the Machos," said Big Mary.

"You're right, Big Mary. But where can we hide?" asked one of the Middle Marys.

"Right! Where is the last place the Machos will ever look for us?" chorused the rest of the Middle Marys.

"I know," said the Littlest Mary, "in the Macho Cave. And everyone stop calling each other 'Mary.'" So they moved into the Macho Cave and did their very best to act Macho, thus inventing Butch.

Longitude L'Attitude

The first thing to do to put yourself on the Butch map is to develop Butch Attitude. While the gay community abounds in Attitude, this is not the correct Attitude for Butch. Gay Attitude is the result of an overwhelming amount of flawless taste with which gay people energetically judge absolutely everything. No gay person has ever been at a loss for an opinion. Butch, on the other hand, is hopelessly taste-free.

Asking gay people to get off their Pedestal of Immaculate Taste is about as easy as asking them to divulge their true age. No one said that becoming Butch would be easy.

The Butch Attitude Blow-job Blow-out

1. Sit quietly and shut your eyes. Get accustomed to the dark. Start to notice your thoughts. Are they engraved? Written in neon? Broadcast over a P. A. system? Splashing across the headlines? Are they French? Trademarked? Cashmere?

   Do your thoughts listen to one another or are they constantly interrupting one another?

2. Imagine that you are a balloon in the exact shape of yourself. You are filled with hot air. Flying around inside are millions of *decoratif* little butterflies. They represent all of your taste. The butterflies flutter around and tickle your skin. This makes you feel mildly carsick, much the same feeling you experience when you walk into a crowded bar by yourself.

3. Now imagine a cute little fairy. He's about three feet tall and his name is Miss Hoover. He saunters up to you, pushes your knees apart, and starts giving you a blow-job. He is sucking all the butterflies out of you.

   You can no longer remember which fork is the salad fork. You can't remember whether madras is in or out. You can't remember who said, "What a dump!" or why it was said. Or whether you've renewed your opera tickets. Or even why you go to the opera in the first place. You can't remember your fabulous quiche recipe.

   And worse, you no longer care.

4. And now imagine that Miss Hoover is so filled with your hot air and butterflies that he may explode. Slowly, he floats up and somersaults away, a dinky dirigible out of control.

5. Finally, imagine yourself deflated. Your body is completely still. You feel nothing. You think nothing. Your breathing is calm. Possibly you are taking a nap.

Welcome to Butch Attitude.

Butch Movement

Born Yesterday

Butch bases his entire charisma upon Butch Attitude. Butch is pure, Butch is direct, Butch is less...much less. The key to developing Butch is simplicity, a quality that does not particularly abound in the gay community.

Many people suffer rather frenetic childhoods and still manifest the traumas in a complex collage of nervous mannerisms. These people are stumbling encyclopedias of psychotic body language. Observing them walk down the street is like watching their depraved childhoods on reruns. Many people are not interested in keeping secrets.

Butch, on the other hand, tells us *nothing* with his body language. Butch has no past, no history; if anyone was born yesterday, it was Butch.

Blinking, Napping, Sleeping & Comas

Let's begin with the most minimal movement. Let's look at Butch asleep. Sleeping is Butch's favorite activity. During sleep, Butch really lets himself go. Here is freedom.

He may occasionally take off his sunglasses.

Butch's bed is located in the center of the room and beckons to him every time he passes by. Butch often lies down in passing. He is fond of staring at the ceiling, gazing at the ceiling, blinking at the ceiling. No hour is too busy that Butch cannot accommodate a nap.

How to Sleep

Do you worry a lot? Do you crawl into bed only to find your day flashing before you while you edit in all the things you should have said? Are you getting tired of trying to balance your checkbook? Did your mother tell you you were special and you wish you could find at least one other gay man who thought so? Are you tossing and turning so fast you're getting carsick?

Did you just jack off twelve times in the hopes it would exhaust you, and you're wide awake and still horny?

This is *not* Butch. If you have attained Butch Attitude correctly, you will not be able to remember what there is to worry about. The mere sight of a sofa sets Butch to yawning. Butch can get up after crashing for fifteen hours, have a cup of coffee, and then go back to bed for a nap.

The trick is to empty your mind sufficiently, and any wink can magically multiply into forty, even in the dentist's waiting room.

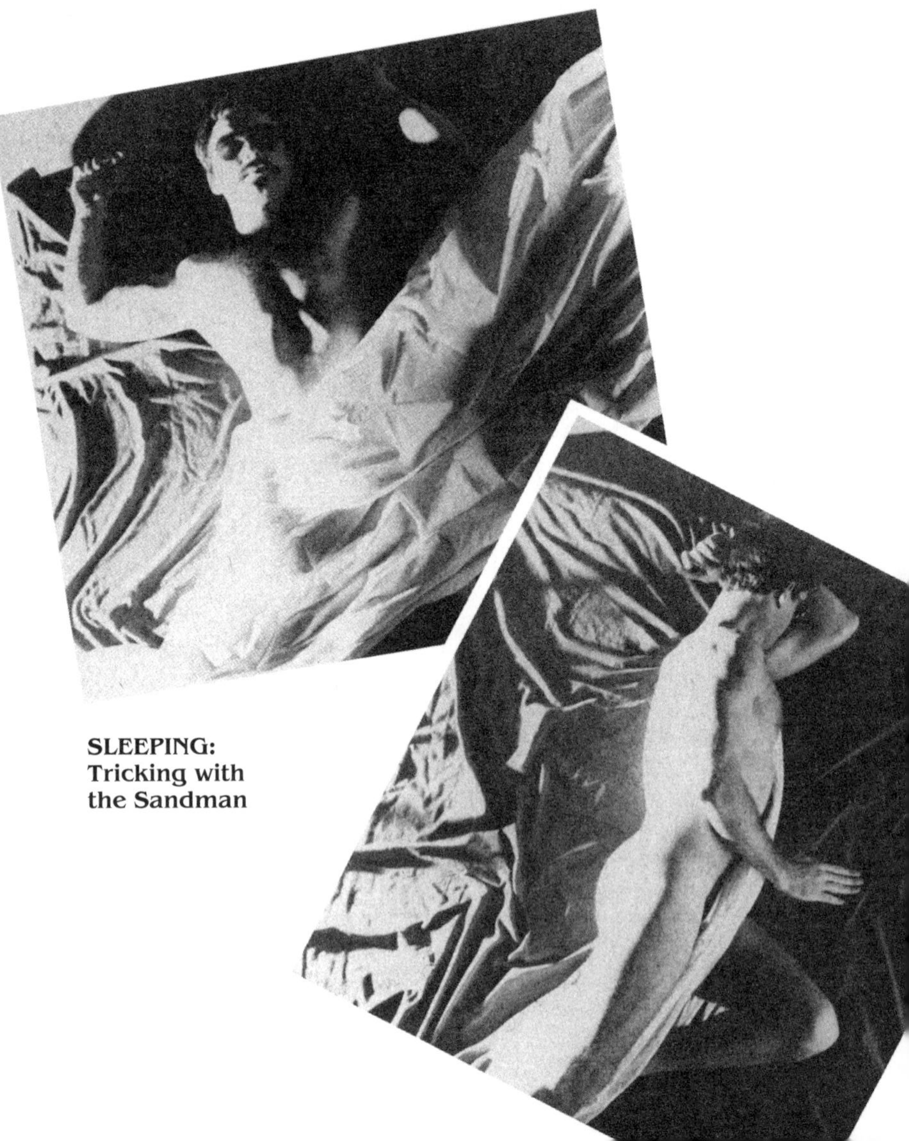

SLEEPING: Tricking with the Sandman

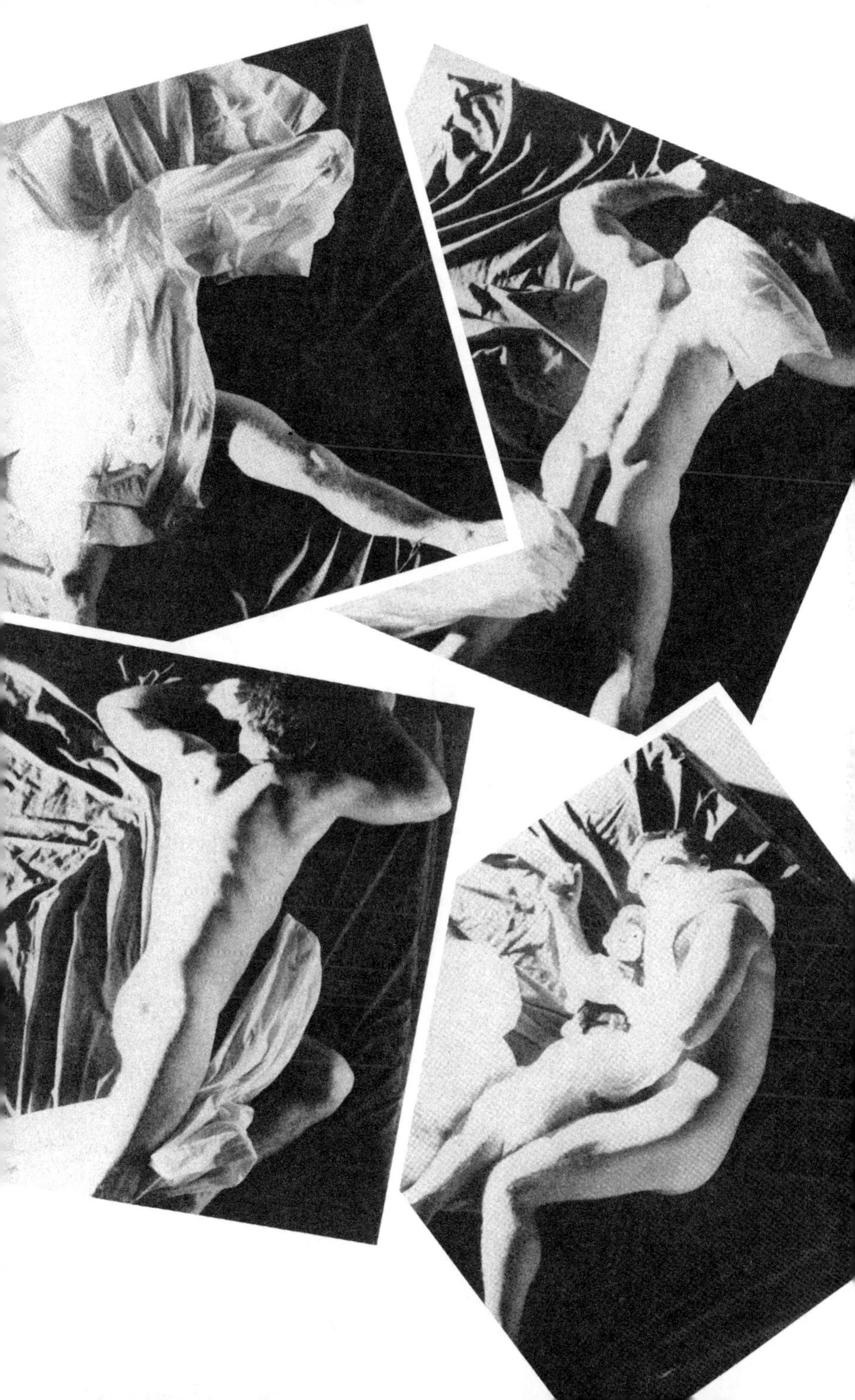

Sitting, if You Must

Of course, the truly Butch thing to do is to stand, but there are places, such as cars, where it is usually more appropriate to sit. It is also extremely difficult to get out of bed without sitting up first, even if for a moment.

These should be your three areas of concern:

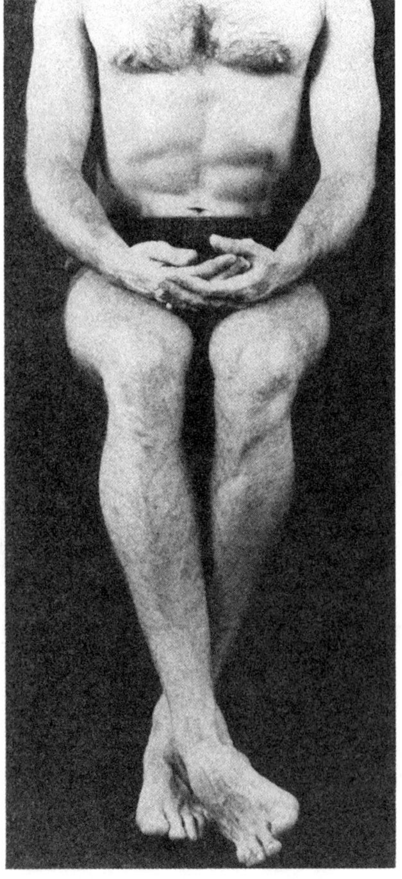

The Back. Scrunch it. Slide your butt forward until you are barely visible, as if to say, "Hey, what's there to see? This is boring." *Do not sit up straight under any circumstances.* Good posture is a sign that the nuns got to you in primary school. Remember: The nuns didn't get to you. No one did. No one ever will. Amen.

The Arms. Cross them. Fold your arms across your chest as if to say, "Hey, so show me something, okay? I'm bored." And should a hot number walk by, you will be able to flex without looking like that's what you're doing. Whatever you do, *do not fold your hands in your lap.* This looks as though you're waiting for your grandmother to serve tea. Remember: You *don't* like tea. You don't *have* a grandmother. You don't have a past.

The Legs. Keep those knees at least a foot and a half apart. *Do not cross your legs—ever!* This is the area of greatest failure in the development of Butch. Leg-crossing is an immediate giveaway of an amateur Butch.

First, try a few exercises.

> Sit with your knees touching. Now place your right ankle on your left knee. Cross your legs at the knee. Keeping your legs crossed, tuck the upper foot behind the lower leg.

Now, how do you feel? Like you're hiding? Like a pretzel? Notice how tying yourself into a physical knot reflects your mental state. Pretzel

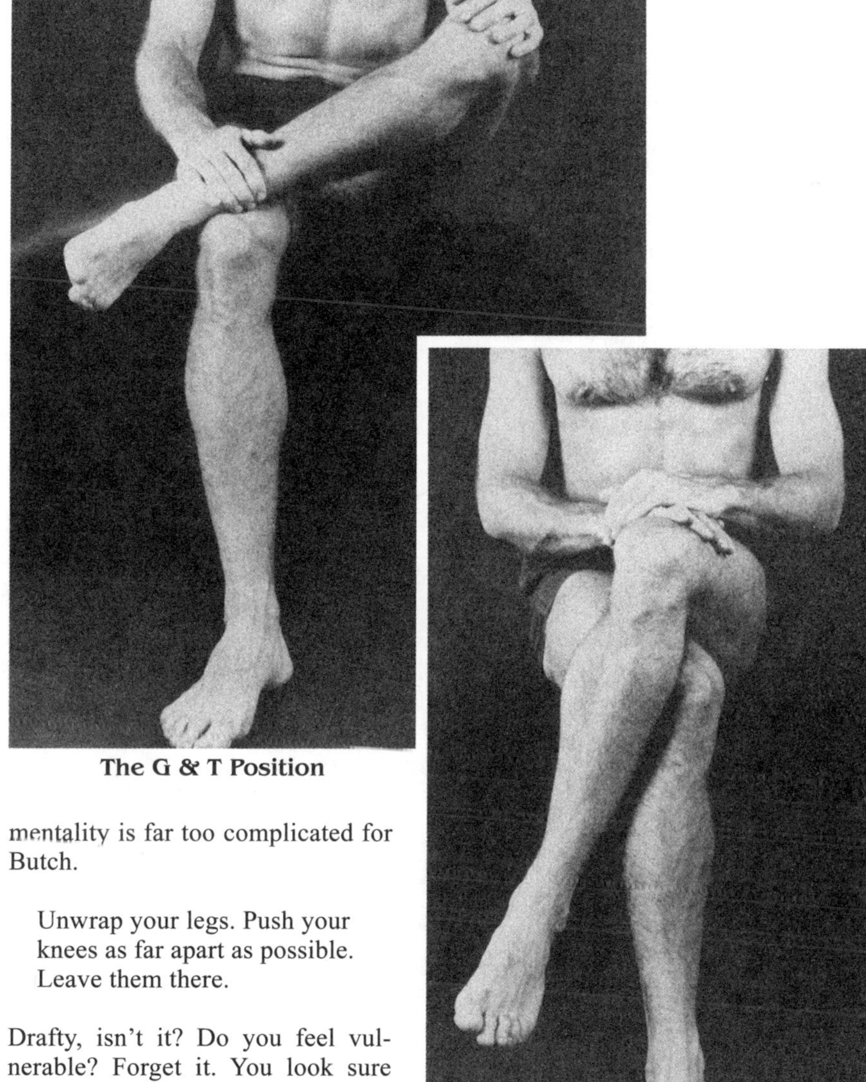

The G & T Position

The Pink Lady Position

mentality is far too complicated for Butch.

> Unwrap your legs. Push your knees as far apart as possible. Leave them there.

Drafty, isn't it? Do you feel vulnerable? Forget it. You look sure of yourself and above penetration. Butch is *always above penetration*. The message is clear: "I have nothing to hide, whereas you...." Butch is great at avoiding all invitations to personal contact and always

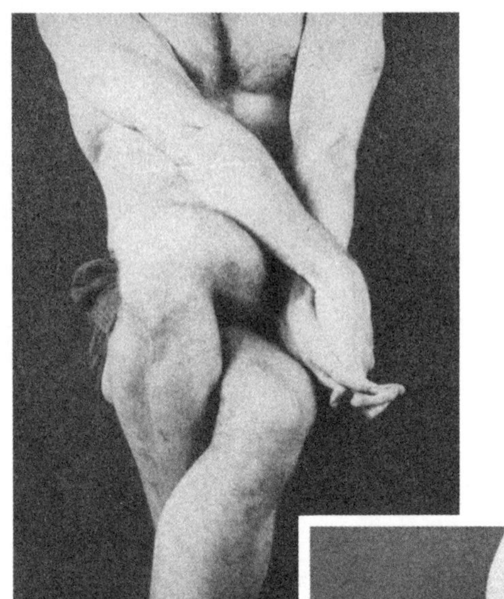

The Shirley Temple Position

manages to throw the ball back in the other person's court before the other even knows it's gone. Keeping your knees as far apart as possible reads only too clearly: "Hey, am I hung, or what? I couldn't cross my legs if I tried. Shit, if I just pushed my knees together I'd probably castrate myself. Man, this equipment has gotta breathe."

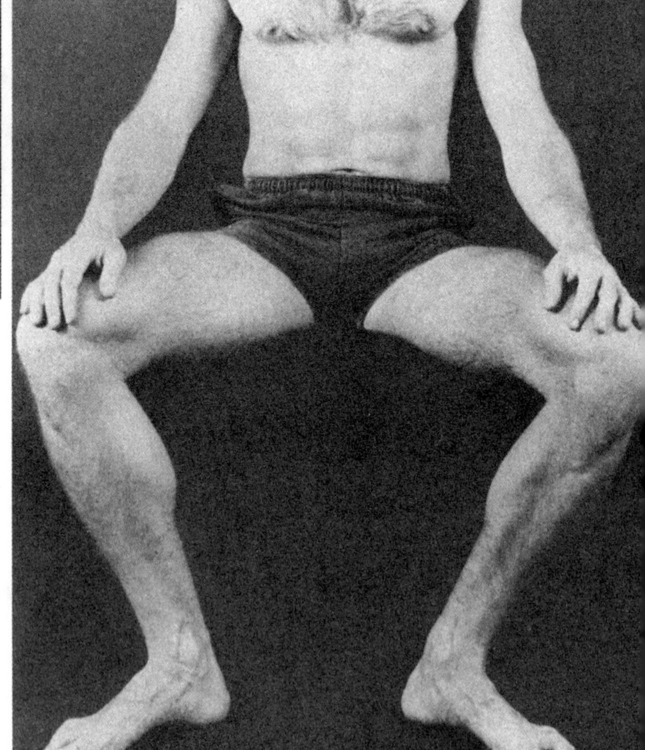

The Budweiser Position

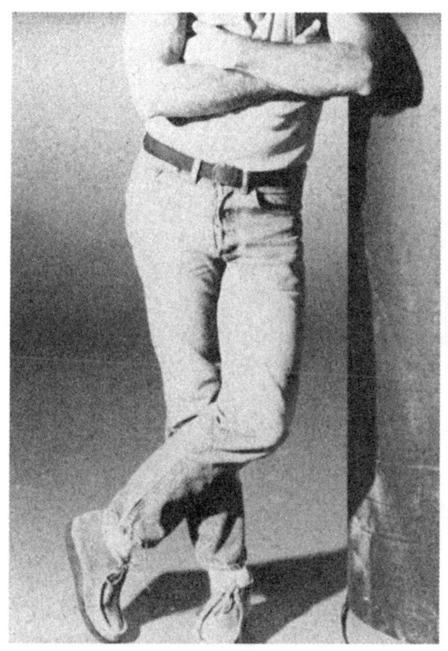
The Side Lean

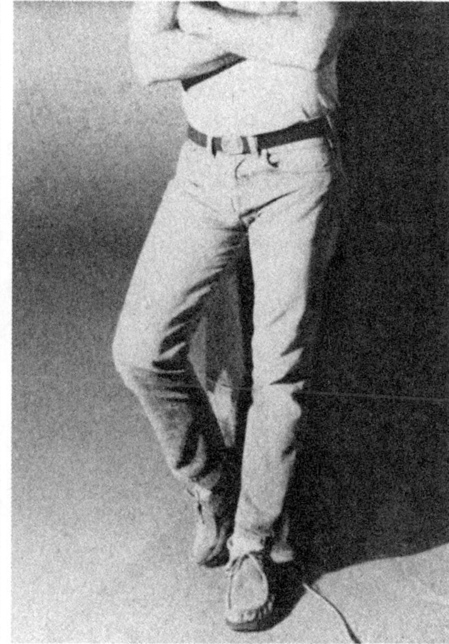
The Back Lean

Standing, Almost

Butch never really stands up... not all the way. He leans. The prevailing attitude is, "Hey, this is boring. Maybe I'll stand up. On the other hand, I'm thinking of taking a nap." Leaning is nowhere as committed as standing, and is much more aesthetic.

There are two popular leaning systems. The Side Lean, derived from the expression "the side lines," is a popular lean when Butch is standing outdoors watching the world parade by. In the side lean, Butch leans against a telephone pole and slowly scans the countryside for wildlife in heat.

The Back Lean, named in honor of "back rooms," is a popular indoor lean. This lean is always a success when Butch is in the throes of drug abuse because Butch can pass out and still remain standing if he has taken the precaution of nailing his shoe to the floor. And this is Butch's favorite sexual position.

While leaning, the arms may be crossed or the thumbs may be hooked through the belt loops. Or put your hands in your pockets and just look like you've got a secret.

One foot is always off the ground. This is a symbolic claiming of one's territory, much in the way that a dog raises his leg near a fire hydrant.

With practice, every Butch develops his own unique lean. Trademark leaning may transcend to an art form: Posing.

The Importance of Chewing While Leaning

Chewing is a subtle body language accent that keeps Butch leaning from looking too laid back. Chewing spices the land of ennui with a hint of energy. What to chew?

You may chew the following:

Gum. Great at the gym. Critique other people's workout by sharply cracking your gum at them.

Toothpick. Mandatory for two hours following each meal. Doubles as a weapon in crowded elevators.

Hay. Hay is for horses, cows, cowboys, Huck Finn—and Butch.

Cigarette. Gives waiting a more businesslike air. Always a hit with a beer in the bar. Not always attractive if you have reached the stage where you are coughing up green phlegm.

Joint. Always an up for a party.

NOTE: If you plan to do a lot of leaning while smoking a joint, be sure to take a test run at walking. Otherwise you may wind up in Butch's least favorite position: flat on your face in public. This may give the wrong idea to potential tricks.

In no way should the lean ever be dominated by chewing, as in the case of nervous mannerisms. Butch is never nervous.

You may no longer chew:

Pencils.

The feathers on your boa.

Your sunglasses.

Your mustache (of course, you may continue to chew other people's mustaches).

Your nails.

Walking, or What Becomes a Legend Most

Walking is another little way Butch reminds the world that he is endowed with legendary features. Since very few people can actually verify this mythology, a prop is needed for practice.

First, walk around normally. Notice how freely your legs move as you glide from one foot to the other. Notice how your hips swing in and out, perfectly counterbalanced, as your shoulders cut back and forth. Notice how the entire flow is set off as the arms swim forward. Notice how you always wanted to be a dancer.

Now, take a large cucumber and push it down one pantleg. Walk. Notice how your Levi's are about to castrate you. Notice how your thighs are cramping and your knees are locked. Notice that your feet are no longer willing to leave the floor, that your hips and shoulders no longer rotate, that your sphincter has tied itself into a macramé sampler. Your arms ought to hang about six inches from your body and your hands should seem to gasp for air. Notice how Boris Karloff imitated this walk to create his most famous Butch character, Frankenstein's monster.

NOTE: Practice the Butch walk until you no longer need the cucumber.

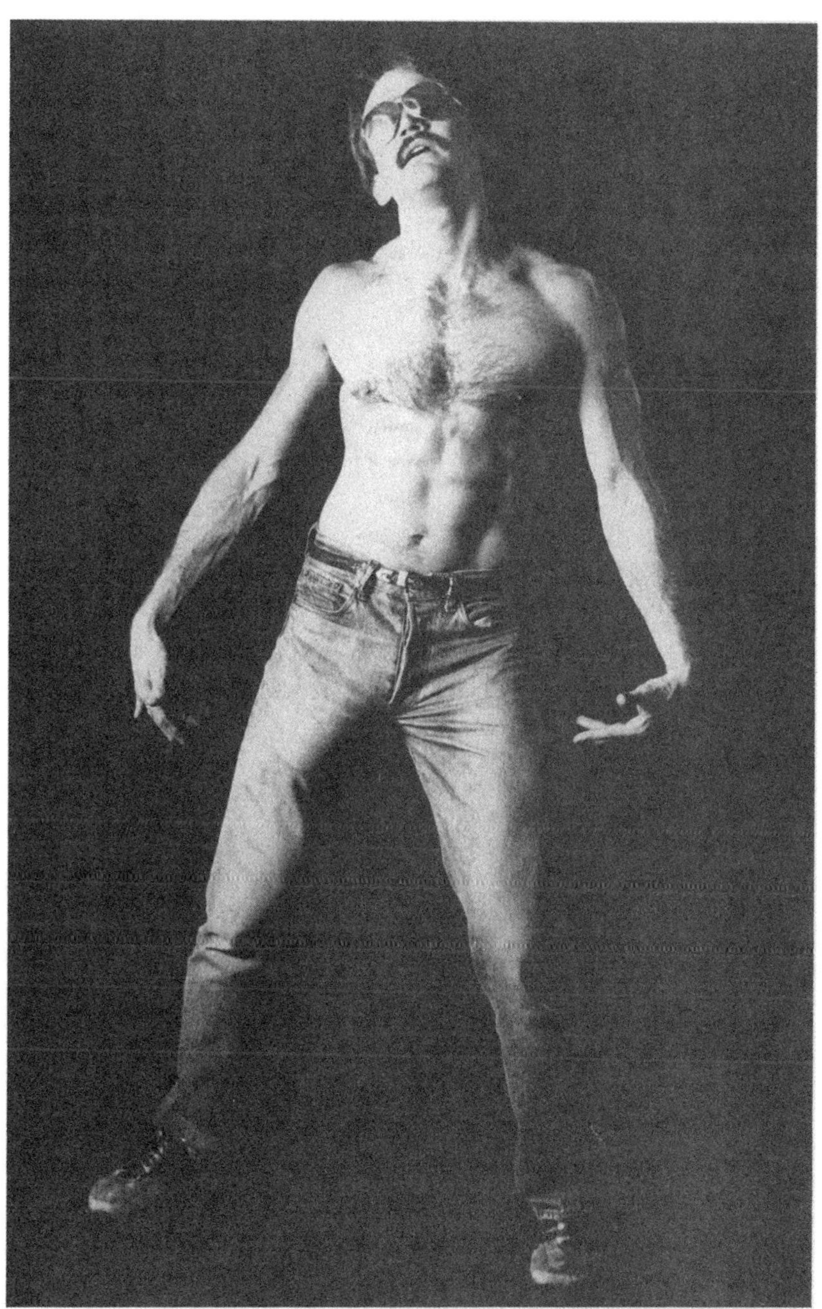

At no time during a practice walk should you attempt to sit down.

The Perils of Carrying Things

Butch is never seen carrying anything. A person bustling down the street burdened by packages appears committed. People who buy packages have lovers and on Christmas morning they do a lot of coke, drink champagne, and open their presents together. Butch is not interested in shopping for presents. He does not make shopping lists, nor does he check them twice. Butch does nothing twice, at least not with the same person. He is not interested in being committed, even if free drugs are involved.

If Butch is asked to hold something, he clutches it like a football. This is perhaps fine for a woman's purse, less good for birthday cake.

Every month or so Butch must carry out his trash. This is usually done late at night, after everyone else is asleep. Or he uses hefty bags, accumulating six months of trash, which must then be dragged, not carried out.

Instead of carrying things in his hands, Butch uses a clever day pack to carry around those items that it would be unwise to be caught without. The day pack is a brilliant cross between a briefcase and a purse, yet sings of the Marlboro Man. It is made of waterproof canvas, and comes in all the Butch colors, from khaki to olive.

Running?

Just where do you think you're *going*? To catch a bus? To get the soufflé out of the oven before it falls? To turn off the water before the bubblebath gets all over the floor? To...

Forget it!

There will *be* more buses; there will be more men. There will, however, be *no more running*! Unless, of course, you happen to find yourself in an Irwin Allen disaster movie—and you won't, because you would have to get up too early.

Butch is never early. Butch doesn't mind being late. After all, what could possibly happen before Butch arrives?

If it doesn't come in a bottle, then there is no RUSH!

Portable Butch: Contents of the Day Pack

- Several extra pairs of identical sunglasses.
- Complete gym outfit in mismatched colors.
- Several jockstraps, yellowed.
- Bathing suit, in case the sun comes out.
- Suntan oil, lotion, cream, and sun screen.
- Vaseline, lube, and elbow grease.
- Small white towel for cleaning up oil, lotion, cream, sunscreen, Vaseline, lube, and elbow grease.
- Several cock-rings, different rings for different moods.
- Clothespins, plan for at least three sets of nipples.
- Snake-bite kit, in case more nipples show up or, God forbid, a snake.
- Dope, a veritable smorgasbord.
- Cigarettes, several packs with two in each.
- Matches, same as above. Covers advertise different bars, thus allowing Butch to flash a variety of sexual whims to prospective tricks.
- Fingernail clippers and an emery board. Butch knows that some people are cruising for more than large baskets.
- Address book. This antiquarian relic was filled up years ago. A rubber band struggles to contain several hundred pieces of paper, all scribbled with hopeful tricks' phone numbers.
- Several bottles of poppers, one broken.
- Aspirin.

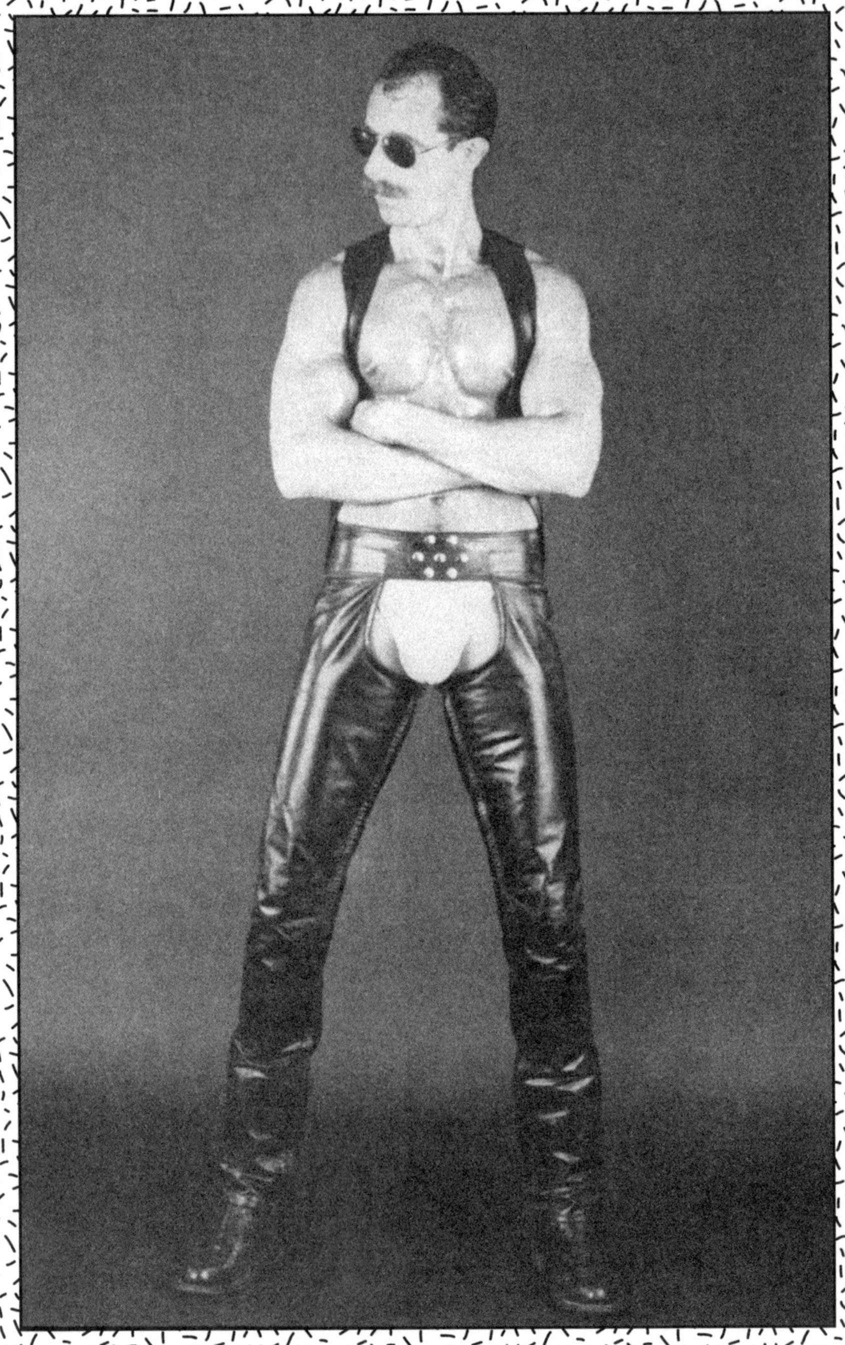

Butch Noises

Talking

Having mastered the art of motion, it is now possible to add sound. And as talkies ruined the careers of many silent screen stars, so talking has nipped the careers of many aspiring Butches. The key to Butch Talk—a point that deserves constant repetition—is simplicity. Why bother to complete a sentence when the sentiment can be conveyed in a phrase?

To comprehend Butch Talk most fully, you must refer to Strunk White's *Elements of Style*, a very slender handbook that manages to make a tedious case for clear, logical, direct, and precise prose. Its incessant pleading could drive many aspiring Butches to the brink of a well-deserved breakdown. Why is this so? Because many members of the gay community thrive on excess. And the gayer areas of town are often knee-deep in exclamation points.

Butch Versus Un-Butch: A Duet

Let's compare how Butch (*B*) talks with un-Butch (*u-B*) talk.

You can immediately see how the un-Butch voice dangles at the end of an irrelevant modifier or hides as an object of anyone else's preposition: *Butch* is always the subject.

u-B: *Mary, this man was so handsome; eyes to lay down and die over, not that it would do any good; eyes that said "I'll call..." but he didn't even try to get in touch with me.*

B: ***I'm not into bedroom eyes.***

Note that, whereas the un-Butch voice is always passive, Butch is always active.

u-B: *Mary, happiness is no longer being sought by me in this lifetime: I'm giving up men.*

B: ***I'm going out.***

Un-Butch talk is utterly prone to the negative voice. Butch always uses positive words; it uses fewer of them.

u-B: *You're out of the Special, aren't you? I knew it! You're not? I don't believe it!*
B: ***Give me the regular.***

This insecurity keeps the un-Butch voice shrouded in vague, indefinite terms. Butch, as always, is concrete.

u-B: *Michael is so busy, but he insinuated that if he finishes his workout early, and his friends don't come into town, and he doesn't do his laundry, which he really needs to do—especially his towels—that he might call if he's around a phone and maybe we'll see about possibly getting together.*
B: ***Mike's full of shit. I'm going to the movies.***

The un-Butch voice dramatically paints mood after mood with excessive adjectives, adverbs, and other descriptive phrases, much like Debussy. Butch, as always a meat-and-potatoes man, sticks to basic nouns and verbs.

u-B: *...Yes, harder, come on, faster, hold it... slide it out, now slowly back in. Come on, deeper harder, all the way.*
B: ***Shit. I'm coming.***

Butch clarity is further camouflaged with u-B refusal to relinquish dramatic, yet totally superfluous words.

u-B: *May I offer you a ride in my $47,000 Mercedes—complete in Navy blue eel-skin, with a television in the glove compartment and a complete bar in the backseat?*
B: ***Get in.***

The un-Butch voice often remains confused, refusing to establish a topic sentence. Loose minds promote loose sentences.

u-B: *Mary, do you see little green elves under this bed? I do. Lots of people have green hair these days. How old are you? The icing flowers were squashed on my birthday cake. I think I'm going to throw up. That dope sure was strong.*
B: ***Was that joint dusted?***

It is extremely un-Butch to taint conversation with exaggeration, although this is often the only way to save a boring conversation. Butch handles this by not starting the conversation.

u-B: *Mary, it was quite simply the last chic orgy on earth. I came a million times!*
B: Same old people. I came once and left.

Exclamation points are always handy for goosing exaggeration to the level of the ridiculous. This involves a certain amount of vocal animation, unfortunately most un-Butch:

u-B: *Mary! Look what you've done to the sauce! You put the lemon juice in too fast! The butter is boiling! It looks like Egg Drop Soup! The brunch is absolutely ruined! Our reputations are curdled!*
B: This mayonnaise looks yellow.

The last token of wisdom from Strunk & White is to "prefer the standard to the offbeat." This is not a cheery note for those gay people whose entire lives, whose *joie de vivre*, whose very *raison d'être*, is the emancipation of the offbeat. While the un-Butch voice may be rich in superfluity, sarcasm, and insecurity, this same flamboyant display of local color prevents it from being Butch.

Tone Clones

Baby's first word is traditionally "Dada." Many gay people's first word is "Uncle." This word is usually delivered on one's back, while a large bully sits on one's chest and tickles one's armpits. Since talking is difficult when one is gasping for air, the "Uncle" produced will be distorted, squeaky, and nasal.

Many un-Butch voices have developed these modulations into festive character accents. Truman Capote may be a great prose stylist, but he would be unacceptable as a candidate for the Butch Hall of Fame.

Butch speaks with a deep voice. You may deepen your voice by the following technique: Yell yourself hoarse into your pillow each morning before getting out of bed. This will give you a deep, raspy, sexy voice. If Lauren Bacall could do it for a bit part, you certainly can do it for yours.

Butch does not convey excitement in his voice. He does not run words together to get attention, as in, "If-you-don't-come-over-to-this-window-right-this-minute-you're-going-to-miss-the-hunk-from-Parcel-Post-and-it-will-be-*toobadfor-you*!" He does not add syllables where none exists, such as "Read My Lips, Ave Maria, Pectorallus and Phallus Most Extremius Majorius to lie down and die over, no problema, made in technicolorama, this-time-I-mean-it, The End!" Nor does he delete syllables in a frenzy, such as "Read 'em, Mar, pecs and dick of death, Fin." And Butch does not raise his voice at the end of a sentence as though asking for permission. Butch does not care whether he has permission.

The Butch Tonal Scale

The un-Butch tone has a little something for everyone. Entire Wagner operas have been condensed into single bars.

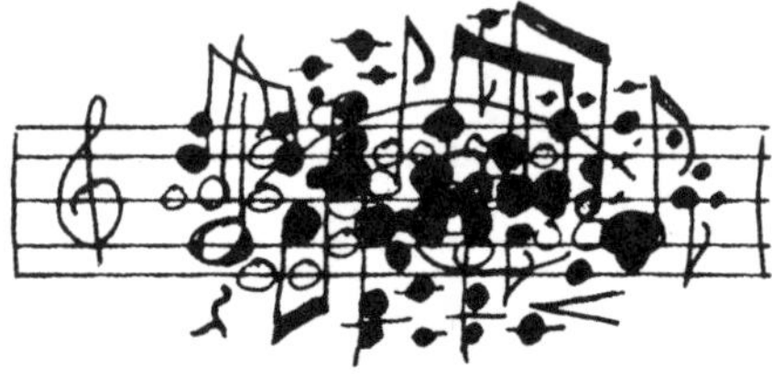

un-Butch

Butch, always a perfect monotone, stands alone between bars.

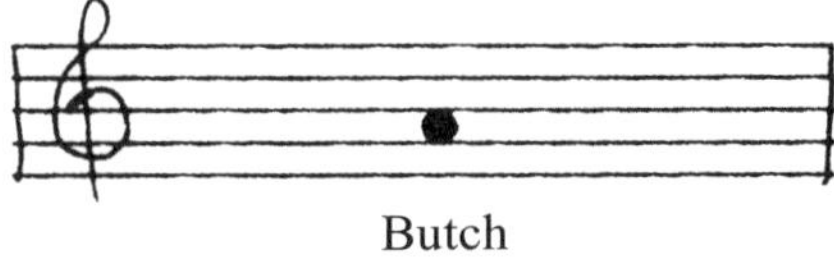

Butch

The Butch Lexicon

Hey!

Because Butch conveys meanings by this sound production, it is perhaps helpful to select a vocabulary. Like Butch this can be honed down considerably.

To assist our Butch linguist attain new heights of simplicity, the word "hey" may be substituted for almost everything Butch has to say. The word "hey" can provide different meanings depending on how it is pronounced.

hey [ha interj. ME. hei, echoic formation akin to Gr. and Du. pronounced softly, whispered]. 1. *Want a toke?* (Asked of someone when your lungs are full.) 2. *Want some poppers?* (To person giving you a blow-job). 3. *Over here, dummy!* (To person looking for you in the bushes in the middle of the night.)

hey [ha! (cut off quickly)]. 1. *Watch it.* (Some bozo is trying to pocket your poppers.) 2. *Get off!* (Some drunkard at the beach trips and kicks sand all over your towel.) 3. *Stop!* (Some fool is walking off with the barbell you're still using.)

hey [ha-yuh (pronounced with a spin)]. 1. *I'm here.* (Light up a new joint.) 2. *Look who's here.* (The trick you couldn't get rid of last night is now sitting next to you at the beach.) 3. *Gotta run.* (Landlord drops by, rent is past due.)

hey [haaa (pronounced with long extended a) (guttural, often used in gutters)]. 1. *Good...* (That's right—pull 'em.) 2. *Better...* (That's right — eat it.) 3. *Best...* (Ride 'em cowboy.)

hey [ha! (fortissimo)] 1. *Bitch!* (Meter maid is giving your motorcycle a ticket.) 2. *Asshole!* (Someone just dropped your coke in the toilet.) 3. *Shit!* (The sling just collapsed, your sex partner is on the floor, your dick has a sudden headache.)

hey [(silent H) A! (the loudest "hey," only used on two occasions)]. 1. *Jesus Christ, fuckhead, have you ever heard of your left-turn signal? I sure as fuck don't have all damn day to sit behind you and your over-achieving Mercedes.* 2. *YOU DIE!* (Delivered with karate chop when someone tries to touch your ass.)

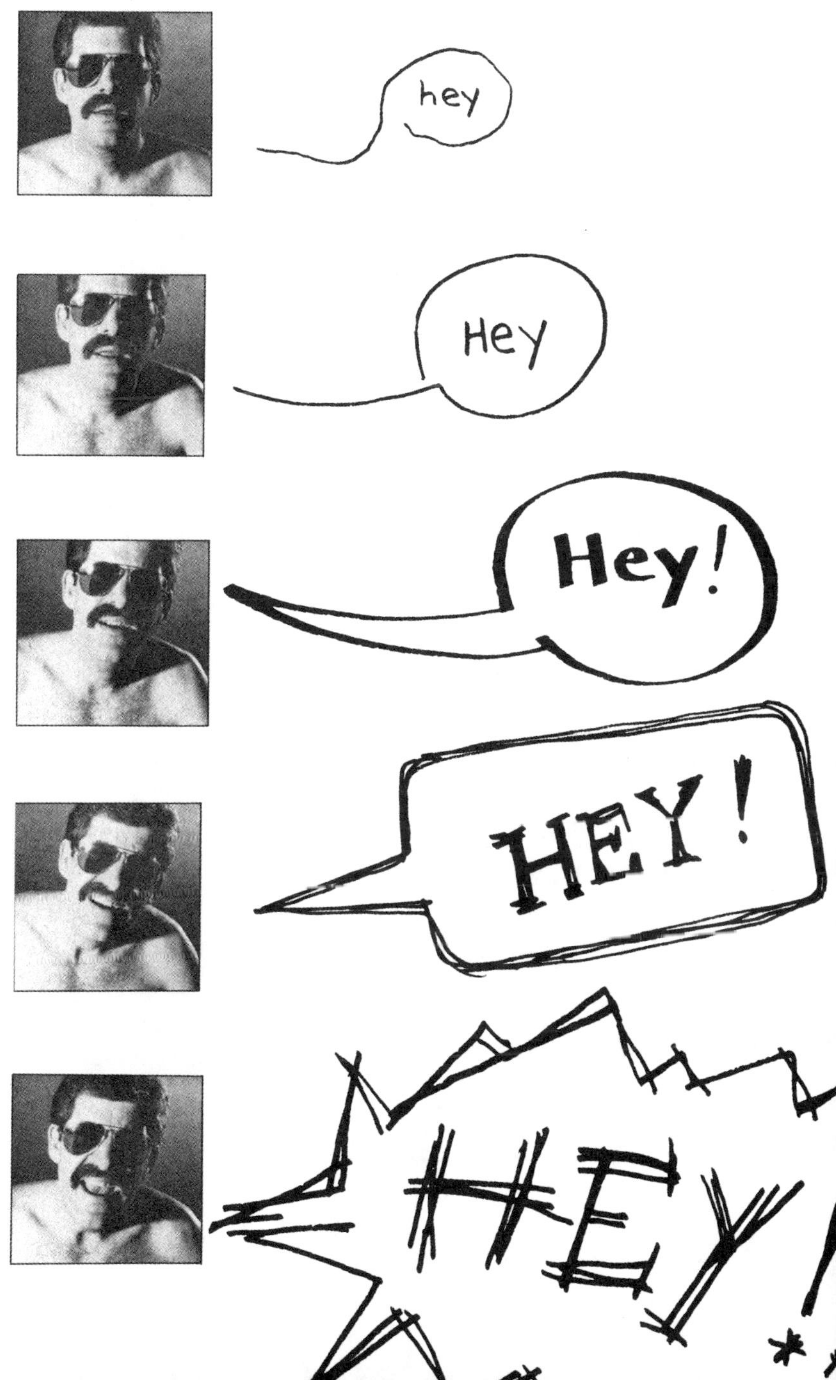
hey
Hey
Hey!
HEY!
HEY!

Butch Music or Usage

Using the Butch Lexicon, fill in the blanks.

____ Jude, don't be afraid....
____ Paula, I'm going to marry you....
____ Mr. Tambourine Man, play a song for me....
____ You've got to hide your love away....
____ Big spender, how'd ya like to spend some time with me....
____ There, lonely girl....
____ There, Georgie-Girl....
____ Joe, where you goin' with that gun in your hand....
____ Little girl, you don't have to hide nothin' no more....
____ Look me over, what do you see?....
____ Good Lookin', what ya got cookin'?....
____ You, get off my cloud!....
____ There, you with the sun in your eyes....
____ We're the Monkeys, people say we monkey around....

Sometimes "hey" is not sufficient. You may actually have to use different words. Since Butch is usually interested in one thing besides himself—men—we will concentrate on "men."

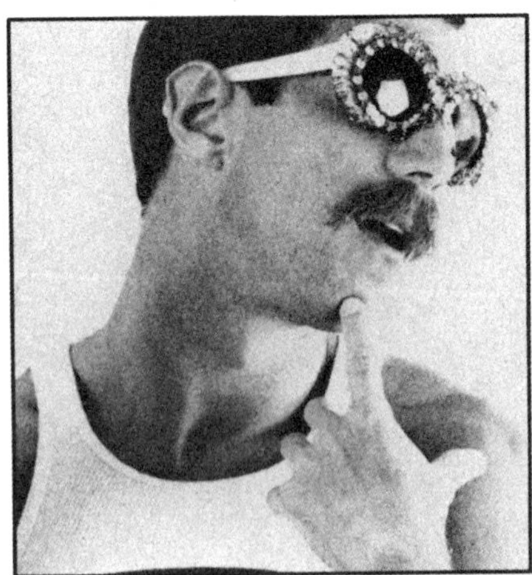
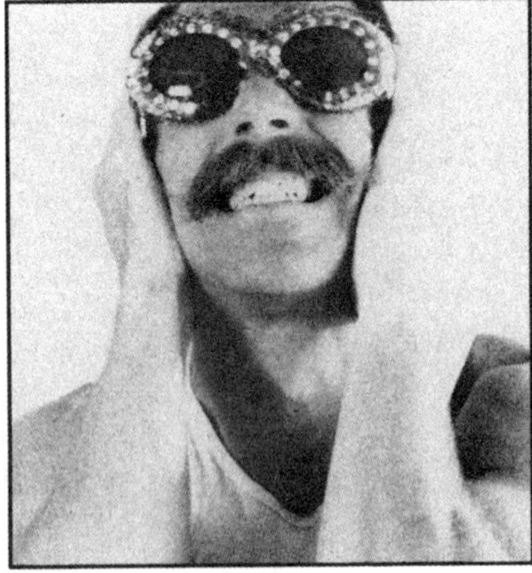

Do not talk with your hands.

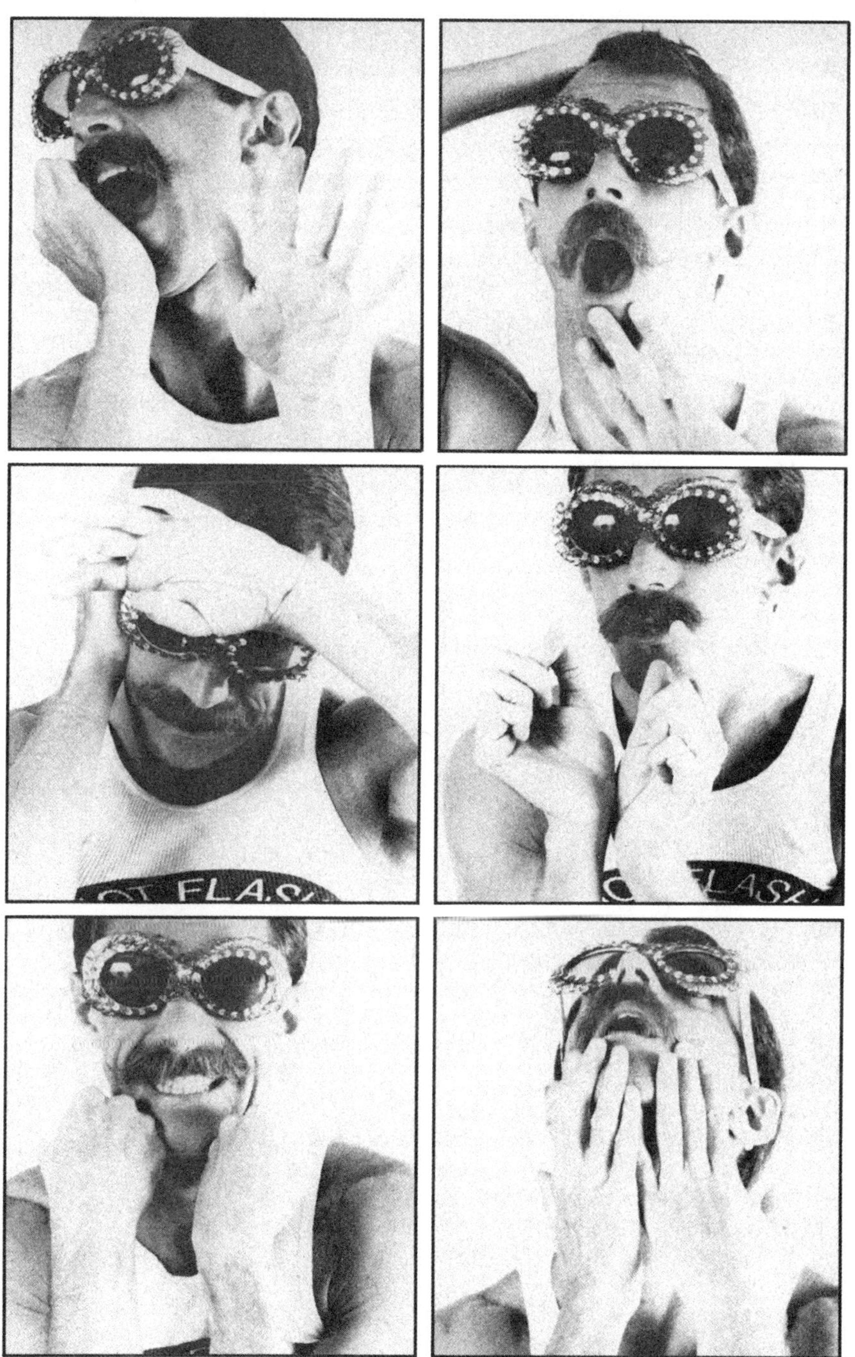

Do not talk with your hands. ***Please.***

What Not to Call Men

It seems that anyone who spends more than five minutes in the gay community comes down with a bad case of gender confusion. This is most un-Butch. The aspiring Butch must cure himself of gender confusion, even if it means taping his mouth shut several weeks. The following rules should answer all questions.

Pronouns. Men are always referred to by the pronoun "he." Whatever you do, no matter how many drugs you're on, no matter how late at night it is, do not call another man "she."

Example: "She was an absolute mess at the tubs last night. Someone was trying to get her to leave a three-way, and they shut the door on her dick."

There are people who will openly admit they are not confused by this statement. These people, however, are not Butch candidates.

Camp Names. The first thing that happens when a man first arrives in the gay community is that he is christened with a camp name. Shrieking out someone else's camp name at a totally inappropriate moment (such as when his parents have just arrived to visit) has provided endless amusement for years. Butch is not amused.

The following camp names *will no longer be amusing*: Blanche, Ramona Rottencrotch, Helen Hairburner, Monica Movinghips, Luella Lipschitz, Wanda Windshield, Mary Motorcycle, Whistler's Mother, Mary of the Cloth, Whichata Yenta, Prunella, Zelda Gooch.

Miss Camp. Camp names for younger people are often preceded with the word "miss." Butch aims more in the direction of "sir." Miss names *to forget*: Miss Claudette Crowbar, Miss Scarlett, Miss Dish, Miss Tan Confessions, Miss Grand Canyon, Miss Thing, Miss Peach, Miss USO, Miss Pickuptricks, Miss Vanilla Moviestar, Miss Rhode Island, Miss Vegetable.

Girls. Just because women are no longer interested in the word "girl" is no reason for the gay community to claim it. Butch will *not* be having "best girlfriends."

Mothers and daughters. After tricking with someone, it is customary to refer to that person as a sister. Someone gay who gives you advice is usually referred to as Mother. This makes the community totally incestuous. When Butch wants to play incest, he will be *Daddy*.

Endearment. Names of endearment are very popular among sisters, and card shops abound in gay communities supported by such affection.

Butch is not interested in sounding like a greeting card, nor is he interested in talking baby talk. He'd rather talk dirty. Terms of endearment *to avoid*: Baby, Babycakes, Babykins, and Baby-oh; Honey, Honeybear, Cookie, and Cookiebar; Doll, Dollbaby, Cutie, Cutie-pie, and Cutie-bear; Sweetie, Sweetheart, and Sweetie-pie; Darling, Tootsie, Frootie, and Zoopie.

Mary. Forget you ever heard the name "Mary."

What to Call Men (If You Must Call Them at All)

Hey guy.
Hey man.
Hey fella.
Hey hunk (leather).
Hey partner (cowboy).
Hey stud (bath house).

NOTE: Adding the word "hot" (the only approved Butch adjective) after the word "hey" may be considered a form of endearment and should be used *cautiously.*

Having mastered the Butch Shuffle and a Perfect Monotone, it is now time to obtain a Butch Body.

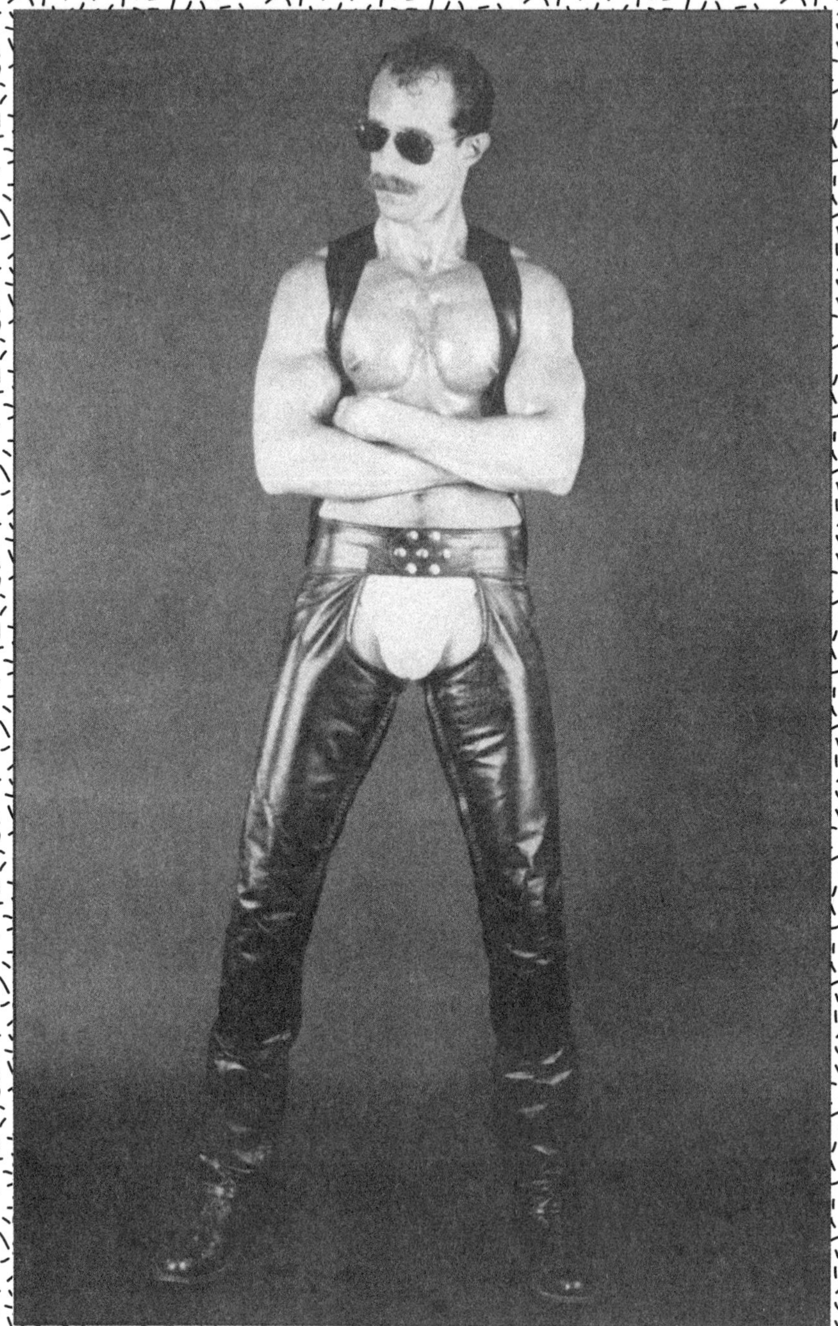

The Butch Body

One rarely gets a second chance at a first impression. On the other hand, if the first impression didn't take, why bother to stick around? Butch does not audition, nor does he rehearse. Every night is Opening Night.

The key to looking Butch is to make a first impression constantly. People say they don't judge a book by its cover. They're lying. People pick up the cover, they judge the cover, they even fuck the cover— without ever opening the book. Butch doesn't care. He *is* the cover.

There is one simple rule in looking Butch: Look hot. Drive men insane. Drown them in their own wet dreams.

No one reads anymore. They just want to look at the pictures.

The Body

There are two types of boys. The first type stayed up late at night jacking off to pictures of mud-splattered pygmy women adorning the pages of *National Geographic*. God only knows whatever happened to these boys.

The second type stayed up late jacking off to pictures of scantily clad Biblical figures found in Janson's *History of Art*. We know what happened to these boys. The Caravaggio fans grew up to be alcoholic queens. The admirers of St. Sebastian grew up with a taste for bondage. And the boys whose eyes kept wandering back to David grew up with a strong propensity for Butch. Hats off to Michelangelo for covering an entire Vatican ceiling with a sensational montage of muscles, nipples, and dicks, thereby planting the seeds of Butch in millions of Catholic schoolboys.

The writing is only too clearly frescoed on those walls. People are looking for a body. People do not want to fuck your car or your Cuisinart or your collection of rare children's books. No one ever said, "I want to fuck that fabulous quiche recipe." So much for breeding.

So butch works out every single day, and has A Body. If Michelangelo were still around, he would have a chain of gyms across the country.

And this would be his recommended work out program:

The Butch Workout Program

The exercises are listed in order of importance. If Butch has dawdled during his workout, he may skip the last few exercises. Remember: Give the people what they want.

As the body is growing into a *pièce de resistance*, there are two body areas that demand special attention. All conversations about men revolve around these two areas.

The Dick

People who write to newspaper advice columns want one question answered: "Is my dick big enough?" No one ever writes wanting to know if their dick is small enough. All men have the persistent fantasy that their sex partners will throw their legs in the air and beg, "Oh, hot man, fill me with that big hot dick." These men worry that this will not happen because their dicks do not fit into the category of "big hot," let alone anywhere else.

The newspaper advisers patiently explain that it is not the size of the penis, but what one *does* with it that counts. If it were strictly a case of a size, everyone could simply run out and buy a large dildo. Or as Maria Muldaur so aptly sang, "It ain't the meat, it's the motion..."

Unfortunately, this woman and the columnists are just trying to be nice.

If you don't have a huge dick, forget it.

Butch does, and no one ever forgets it. Gay magazines are published

EXERCISE	BODY PART
Bench press flies (warm up)	Chest
Bench press barbell	Chest
Incline dumbbell	Chest
Decline flies	Chest
Cross-the-bench stretch	Chest
Pulleys	Chest
High pec press	Chest
Pec compounds	Chest
Adjusting weight on locker-room scale	Arms
Washing hair in shower	Shoulders
Sitting up after benchwork	Stomach
Walking from the gym to the car	Legs
Turning key in ignition	Wrist

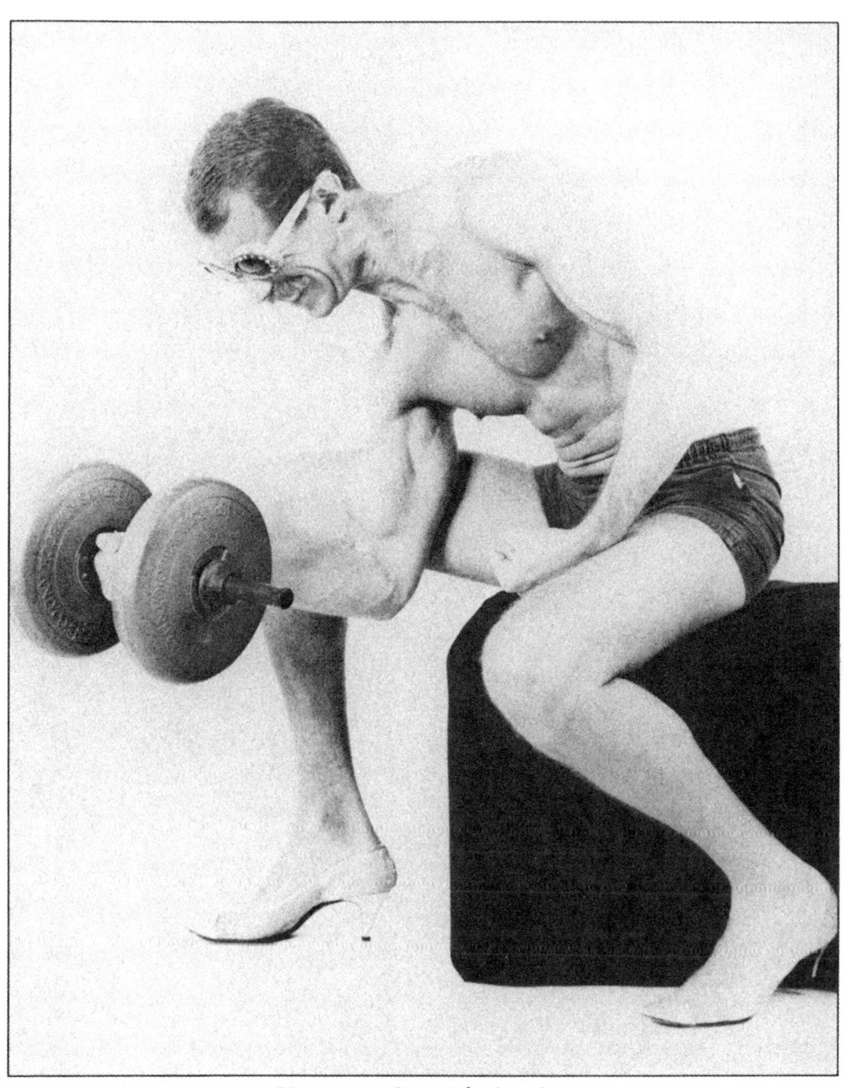

Never work out in heels.

almost entirely on the revenues collected from advertisers who swear they have a product that will make your dick bigger. These people are pulling your leg, not mention what they're doing to your dick. There is *no way* to make your dick bigger. Prayer wouldn't hurt, of course. Neither would lots of exercise.

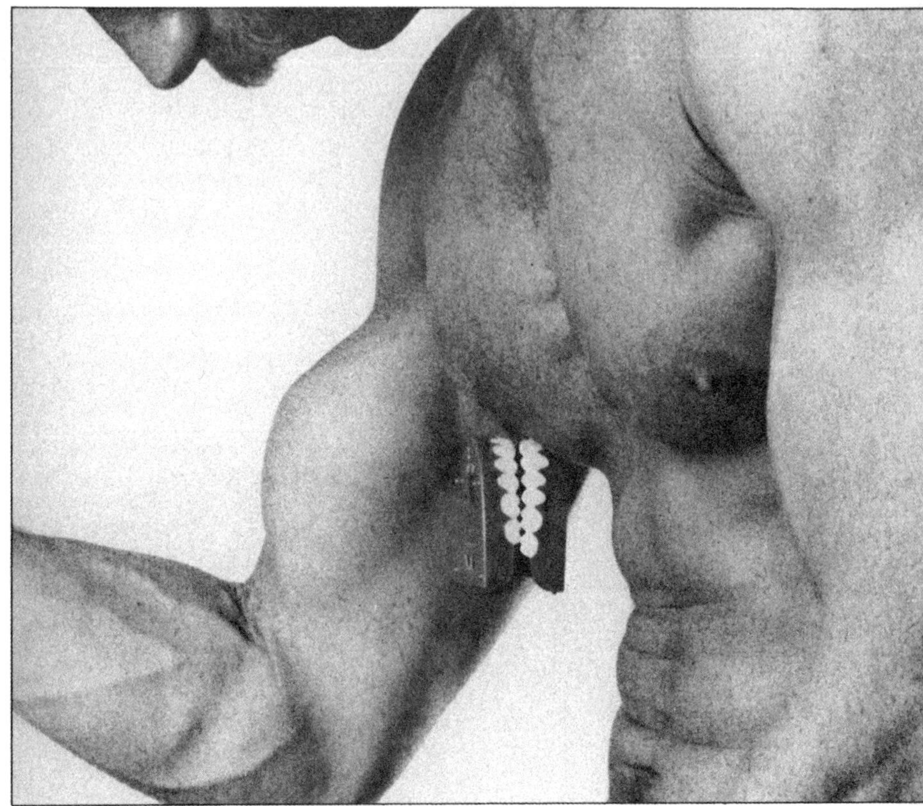

NIPPILIZATION: It's just like masturbation. If you can't find someone to help you out, you can always do it yourself.

The Nipples

There is nothing that gets the natives quite so restless as two luscious nipples figure heading two voluptuous pectorals. Foreplay is back in fashion, and sensitive nipples are having all the fun. Butch's nipples are so sensitive that they get aroused when he is tucking in his T-shirt.

Do you have the kind of nipples that are hard to locate? When you tweak one, does it yawn? The sad truth is that nipples must be broken in, literally as well as figuratively. Someone has to maul your tits to the brink of disaster. It's not a pretty story, but look at the alternatives. Do you want to stand on the sidelines while everyone else is tweaking their way to Nipple Heaven?

Don't despair. Drugs and painkillers are in the same family. You won't feel a thing. The next morning, however, you will wake up to the sound of your nipples screaming, "The top sheet is too heavy!" Tell them to cool it. Tell them to rejoice they are finally feeling something. Then treat them with a generous coating of Neosporin ointment and Vitamin E cream. When the scabs fall off, you'll be a new you.

The Head (And How to Hide it)

The head is covered with features that constantly express emotion. This is disturbing for Butch because he does not like having his emotional barometer read by every stranger he passes on the street. People who constantly ask how you're feeling are usually manic-depressives involved in group therapy. Butch almost always feels the same thing; nothing. Butch is a rock. An austere rock.

One way to guarantee austerity is to camouflage all facial features.

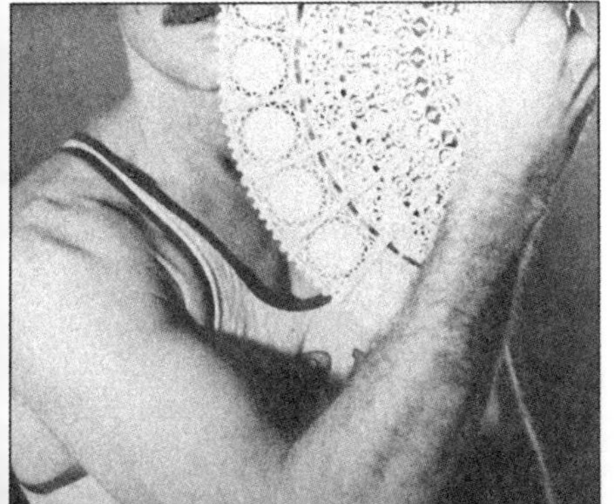

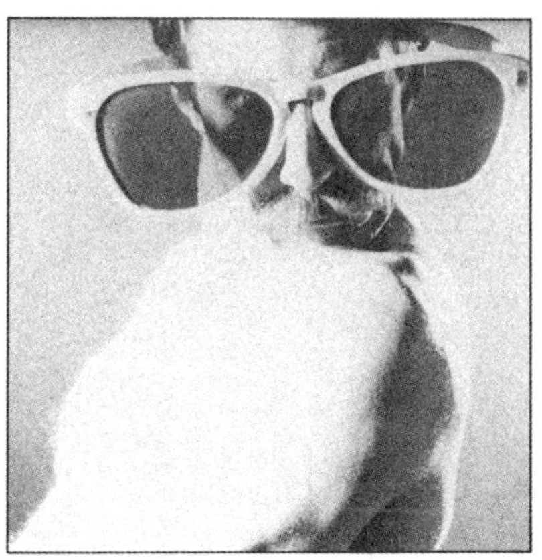

The Eyes

People sometimes wonder how gay people can pick one another out in a crowded room without saying anything. It's all in the eyes. Several split-second glances can convey volumes of pertinent information: "Well, hello, Hot Stuff. Is this gallery opening boring enough for you?" "Yes, I see the hunk over there with the tattoo. Alas, he's straight." "Live around here? Terrific! I just happen to have some real amyl in my pocket. Let's go."

Butch is no longer interested in playing "I.M., R.U.?" with every horny Fairy he happens to meet. Butch is not excited about having other people window-shopping through his soul. Butch wants to play "R.U.? U.R.!" Butch is a peeping Tom. He wants Venetian Blinds.

Thus, Butch wears sunglasses twenty-four hours a day. Butch without sunglasses is like sex without poppers.

The sunglasses are mirrored.

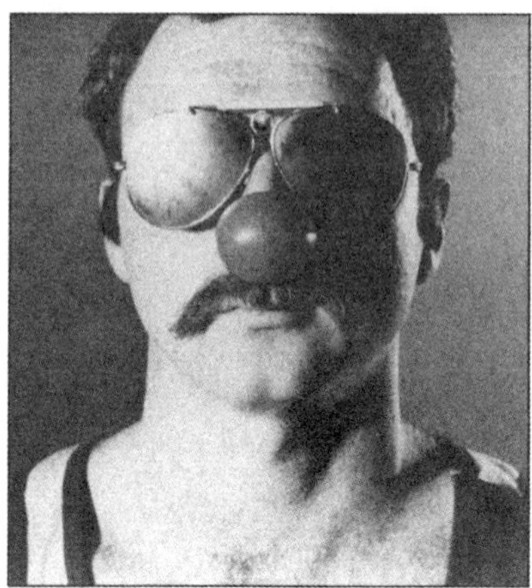

This way not only can Butch remain hidden, but he can constantly distract any person trying to talk to him.

It might also be a good idea if the sunglasses were bulletproof. A mature queen can shoot glances that kill.

The Mouth

Smiles are considered socially acceptable on babies. Smiles on gay people are considered desperate. A smile is an open invitation for rejection. The Butch safeguard against an accidental smile is a large mustache and a beard.

Certain celebrated Butches are known by their unusual cultivation of facial hair. Not too unusual, however.

The Ears

The ears redden during embarrassing situations and may hinder an otherwise stoic response. Since gay life can be one continuously embarrassing situation, Butch has taken the precaution to camouflage his ears. Walkmans are rapidly replacing earmuffs, especially during the summer months.

Hair used to cover the ears, but the current trend is for short hair that no longer reaches the ears, except on men inhabiting small pockets oblivious to fashion, like the first floor of Bloomingdale's and most of Southern California.

The earring is the perfect decoy. Diamonds may be little, but they are not subtle. Neither is chartreuse enamel inlaid with orange coral. Decoys should not jangle, dangle, or in any other way attempt to make noise. It is not subtle to pierce the same ear seven times.

The subtle Butch decoy is the gold stud. A small gold loop may be worn to costume parties, and a skull and crossbones is festive with lots of leather.

Hair

There is no right look for Butch hair. There are, however, lots of possibilities.

Salt and pepper is the ideal color for Butch hair, although black or brown will do in a pinch. Blond is extremely wrong, unless closely crew-cut, unwashed, and covered with motor oil. It is also completely unacceptable to dye your hair. Blonds are trapped outside the realm of Butch except in special cases, but they don't seem to care as they always seem to be having more fun doing whatever it is that blonds do.

On the other hand, light streaks are always fashionable because they sing of the outdoors. Mother Nature cleverly put salt in the ocean and chlorine in the pool to help you. Her kid sister, Miss Clairol, is a no-no.

Receding hairlines, thinning hair, and baldness are all great Butch hair because they make you look distinguished. A full head of hair will pass, unless it is flaunted.

There is *no such thing* as a natural-looking toupee. When people run their fingers through your hair and discover it has the texture of a dead animal, they are prone to run off screaming. Bald is always better.

If you have a bald spot, do not grow the hair around your ears long and then shellac it over the bald spot. This is not amusing, let alone Butch.

AN IMPORTANT NOTE: The One and Only Time to Use a Hair Dryer: Occasionally Butch may wear a pair of white pants during a particularly warm summer evening, or a pair of white cutoffs during a hot spell. Because Butch does not wear underwear, he runs the inevitable risk of spotting himself after taking a leak. This occupational hazard is soon remedied with the use of a hair dryer on medium heat.

That was medium, not high.

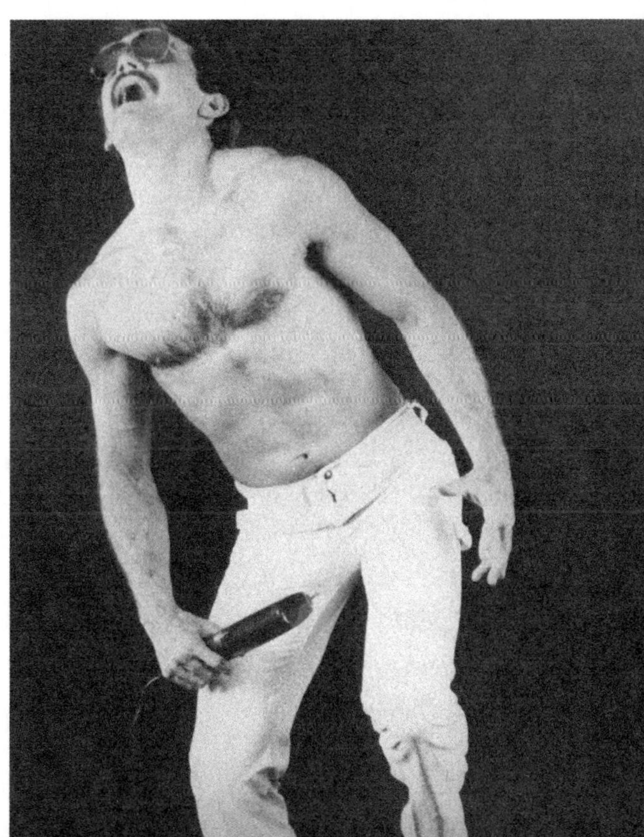

The only Butch use for a hair dryer. (That was medium heat. Not high.)

Facial Hair Types to Avoid

The Hippie Beard. Organic people often store sprouts in their beards. They take mescaline and listen to God. God tells them it is unnatural to make their beds, clip their hedges, or trim their beards. Hippies are going with the flow, which is not flowing Butch.

The Mental Institution Beard. It is not usually a good idea to trim your beard while on drugs.

The Leather Beard. Some members in the leather gang like to trim every hair in their beard to exactly 1/16 inch. This then matches their haircut, so they can look as though they are wearing velvet motorcycle helmets with straps.

The Designer Beard. A little natural gray in a beard is great. But a blond streak? In Southern California they think they can get away with anything!

The Butchest possible combination is a decorative mustache and a two-day-old beard, which suggests that you just came back from shooting the rapids on the Salmon River or from a long weekend at the baths. This look can be continuously cultivated by sticking pieces of cardboard at each end of your razor, which will prevent you from getting a close shave.

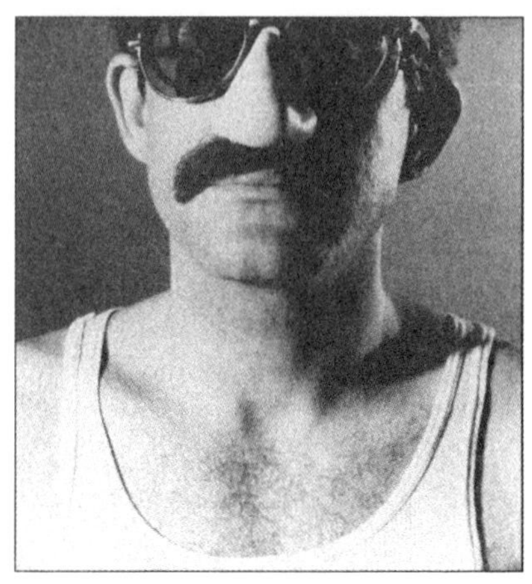

The Nose

There is no clever way to disguise the nose.

Certain people have tried, with nose warmers, Halloween masks, and Groucho glasses. But after a few months, people generally get suspicious.

Luckily, the nose conveys very few emotions.

Butch Dressing

The key to dressing Butch is to enhance what Butch spent a great deal of effort developing at the gym. In no way should Butch's greater attributes *ever* be obscured by clothing.

Pants (Or Panting Baskets)

Butch wears pants that show off his bulging calves, his tantalizing thighs, his perfect buns, and of course, his notorious basket. There is only one pair of pants that can fill all these requirements: Levis 501s. This means straight legs, buttons in the crotch, and a watch pocket.

The Levis you buy will have very little to do with the Levis you will be wearing. New Levis have no shape and feel like raw canvas. You should buy them at least two sizes too large in all directions. You must then carefully shrink them to show off your own perfect personal set of statistics. The result will be a pair of pants that fit like a second layer of skin and feel like old velvet. Someone once said that a well-worn pair of Levis makes the entire lower body feel like the head of a cock, which is not surprising, considering the number of Levis that lead active sex lives. Inexplicably, Levi-Strauss has not yet highlighted this point in an ad campaign.

The 501 Open-button Question

Levis with buttons are preferred Butch style because they assure easy access even while peaking on drugs, and there's never any problem with catching pubic hair, which so easily happens in zippers. It is customary in the gay community to leave *one* button unbuttoned, and there has developed a major debate about *which* button.

The Second-button School. This was the original button to leave open, and clearly asked, "I.M., R.U.?" in crowded elevators where everyone is supposed to be looking at the floor. But this subtle sign has been lost in the flood of more flamboyant advertising techniques such as key rings, colored hankies, pierced nipples, and stuffed bears. Butch, however, does not need to advertise.

The Top-button School. This button is popular with the twenty-nine-inch-waist set because they can leave the button undone and the pants do not pull apart to reveal even minor midriff. These people have recently lost weight. Butch has never been concerned with his weight.

The Bottom-button School. Leaving this button undone says, "Hey, man, my basket is so big I can't even shut my fuckin' pants." It also makes ball-scratching easier. This is the button for Butch.

How to Wear-in Your 501s

1. Fill the bathtub with hot water. Pour in an entire bottle of fabric softener.
2. Put on your 501s; get in the bathtub.
3. Scrub your 501s with Ajax. This will loosen the color and help work out the stiffness. Do not panic when the water starts to turn blue.
4. Stand up and rinse in the shower. Wash off the Ajax, the fabric softener, and the excess blue dye.
5. Go outside and walk around in the 501s until they are dry. The pants will shrink to your gently flexing legs. It is a good idea to save this for a warm, sunny day.
6. Once back inside, observe exactly where your cock rests against your 501s. Trace around the area with a piece of chalk.
7. Take off your 501s and use an emery board to rub the area within the perimeter of the chalk. This will rub out more blue dye and will lighten the area. (This also draws the eye to the crotch and says, "My dick is so big it's wearing a hole through my pants.")
8. Wash your 501s a dozen times. Do not use bleach or the pants will spot and you'll be the laughingstock of your neighborhood.
9. Fold them or, better yet, throw them on the floor of your closet. Never hang them. Never *never* press them! Who do you think you are, Calvin?

BREAKING IN 501s

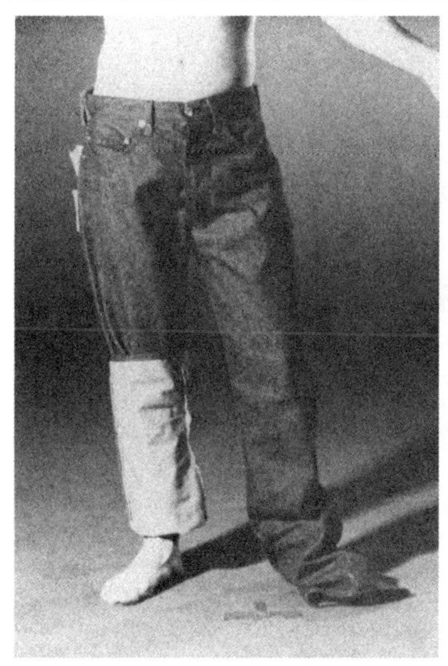

Before

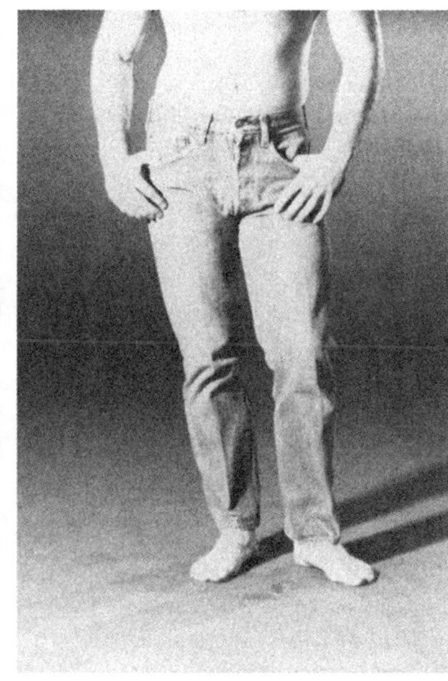

After

Shirts (i.e., Tit-framers)

Butch would prefer not to wear a shirt. Unfortunately, the laws are often archaic, and restaurants always insist their clientele be properly attired. This means, in the minds of obviously mindless legislators, a shirt. But the law does not say that it has to be one of those Brooks Brothers button-down numbers so roomy you could shoplift a sports car inside it.

Butch selects his shirts with one aim in mind: to show off his torso. Michelangelo would have an orgasm just standing around a typical gay bar.

Every Butch shirt has its own particular style, statement and usage:

T-shirts. Butch has several thousand T-shirts. His brand is Jockey's Super Brute, which, although it pops out of the dryer looking like a confused sock, contours the body like spray paint.

Tank tops. As the summer months approach, Butch packs away his T-shirts in mothballs and gets out the tank tops. These are either worn tightly, to broadcast stomach definition, or worn loosely, which allows the nipples to play "Hide 'n' seek."

Gray athletic shirts. This is a Butch specialty and only comes in the Butch color: gray. The shirt hugs the pecs and then flutters loosely over the stomach, ending a few inches short of the gym shorts.

Bowling shirts. It's sporty, greasy, fifties, and Punk. It is also formal. Always rip off the top buttons and roll up the sleeves. Ripped and stained armpits add enhancement.

Hawaiian shirts. It's outdoorsy, greasy, thirties, and a little bit of Paradise. This shirt should never be worn more than once a year. All buttons must be ripped off and the shirt never tucked in. The shirt should be an original brand so that colors have faded for fifty years. Great-looking soaked in sweat.

Blue-denim work shirts. The sensual delight of denim may now wrap the entire body. A decal over the pocket should say "Chuck." The back of the shirt should advertise a garage. Wash the shirt with a bottle of fabric softener and two quarts of motor oil.

Flannel shirts. It is difficult to show off the body in this shirt and it should be worn only when Butch feels extremely confident or is on a date. If Butch should suddenly find himself alone and horny in a flannel shirt, he will go into the nearest rest room and rip off the sleeves.

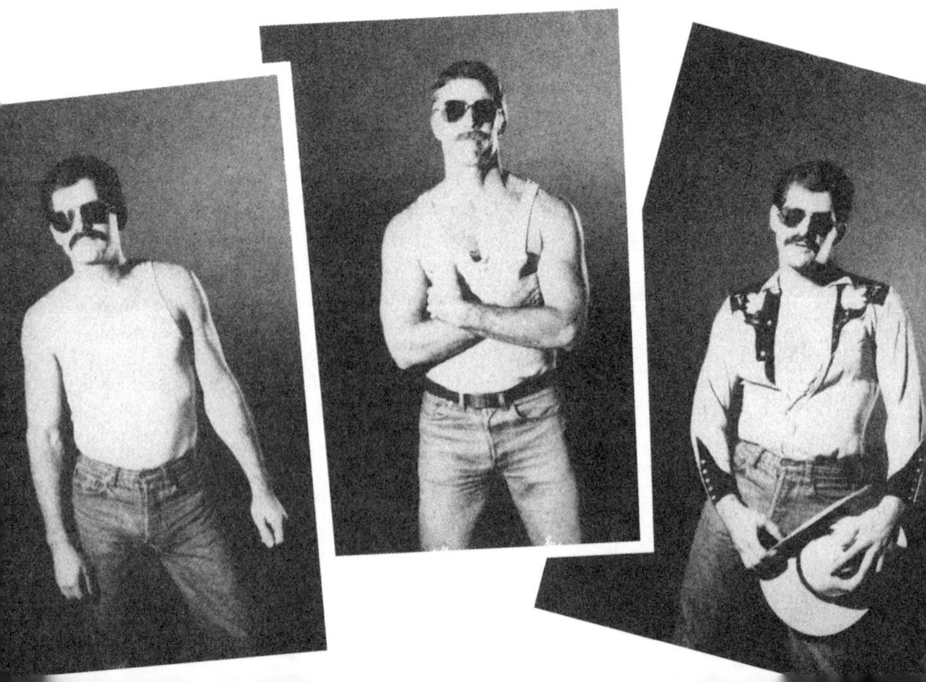

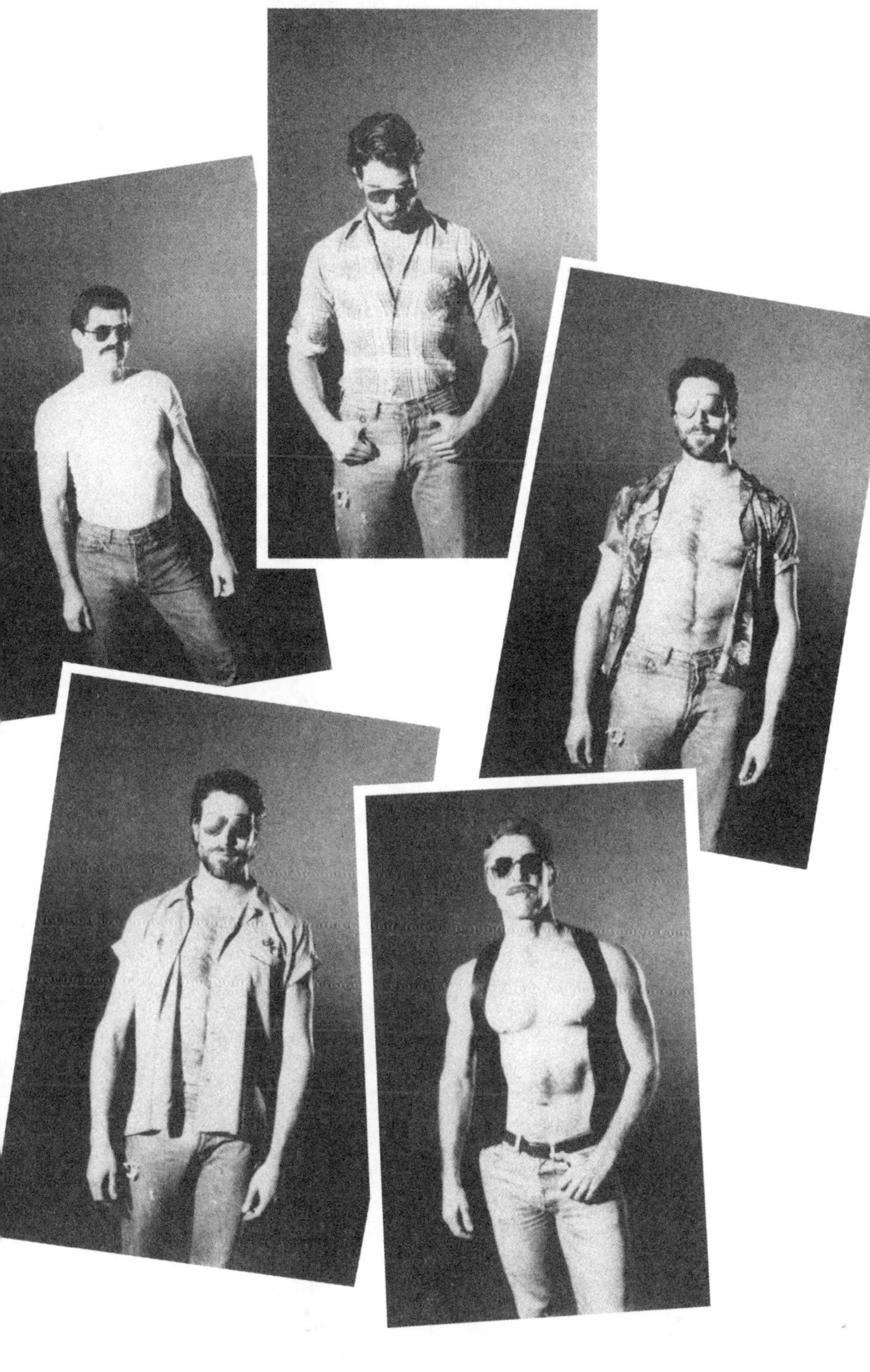

The Chemise Lacoste Dilemma

There was a time when Chemises Lacoste were great shirts. Perhaps they were a little too preppy, but they were 100 percent cotton, and they had that great long flap in back and it never came untucked. That was in the good old days when Lacostes still came from France.

Now Lacostes are made everywhere. Fifteen minutes from wherever you are, there's a little factory huffing and puffing, madly spewing out millions of little alligators. It is difficult to determine what the current fabric is made of—old, moldy, Nichols and May record album covers, perhaps.

So the question arises: What is the Butch solution to a closet full of old Chemises Lacoste, all with one foot in the grave.

And Butch responds: Put the other foot in the grave. If the shirt looks like hell, you can wear it and no one will recognize it. First, rip off that fucking alligator. Then:

- Rip off the sleeves.
- Wash it in bleach.
- Line the birdcage with it.
- Put it on kitty's rug scratcher.
- Wrap meat in it and throw it at the dog.
- Polish furniture with it.
- Use it for a potholder.
- Tie it on the axle of your car and go for a drive.
- Use it as a trick rag.

Or, if you no longer care whether your shirt stays tucked in, you can use it to re-cover the seats in your car and bid *adieu* to Chemise Lacoste.

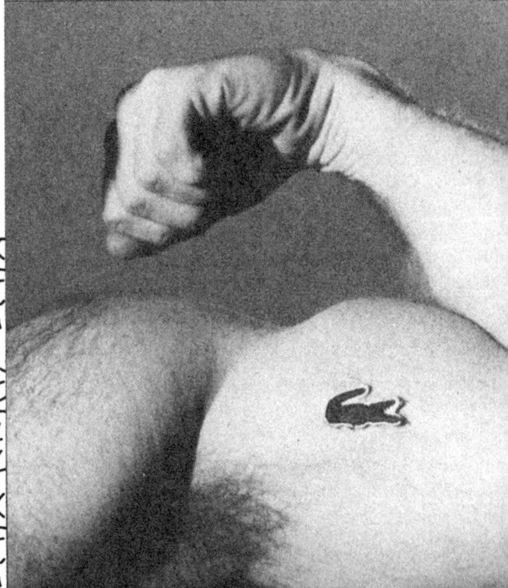

Talking T-shirts

People who have a hard time remembering the ends to jokes often wear T-shirts to help them. There are three different talking T-shirt categories, and three different reasons why Butch would never be caught dead in them.

The Humor Category

Examples: Not a Well Woman
Surrender Dorothy
Ward, I'm worried about the Beaver
Who the hell is Rula Lenska?
Madness takes its toll

Did you ever hear a joke told a second time? A third time? A sixty-fifth time? Did you ever notice that when you are buying a T-shirt, it is sitting on a pile of other T-shirts that are all just like yours? Butch does not care about the Beaver and he doesn't know who Rula Lenska is.

The Sex Commercial Category

Examples: In Heat
Scratch 'N Sniff
Mustache Rides —5¢
With Lipstick—6¢
I like to watch
Yes Sir

This employs the same tactical maneuver that keys, handkerchiefs, and pierced body parts have indulged in: promises. Butch doesn't want to *hear* about it: he wants to *see* it. People who wear T-shirts that say "Yes Sir" and then stand around a bar waiting for Santa to come would do far better if they got down on their hands and knees and started licking boots.

The Bragging Category

Examples: I am a model
Bi-Coastal
Ferrari
Show business is my life
Pines '76 (it's funny how you never see a "Grove" T-shirt)

People who are famous never have to tell other people that they are famous. Ditto fabulous. Ditto Butch. Someone wearing a "Butch" T-shirt will most likely also be wearing turquoise jewelry.

Call me bitchy. Just don't put it on my T-shirt.

SILENCING A TALKING "T" FOREVER

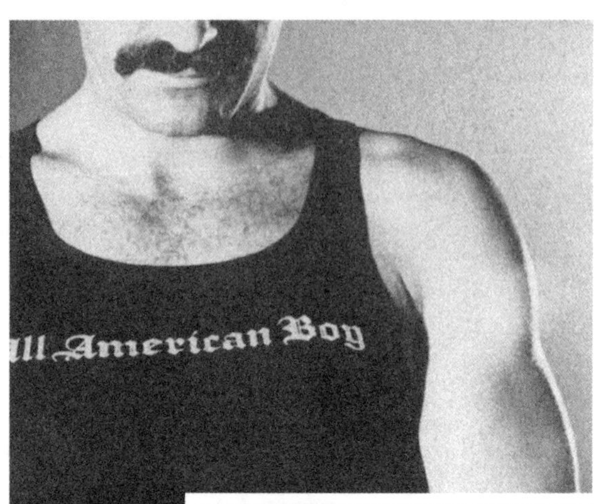

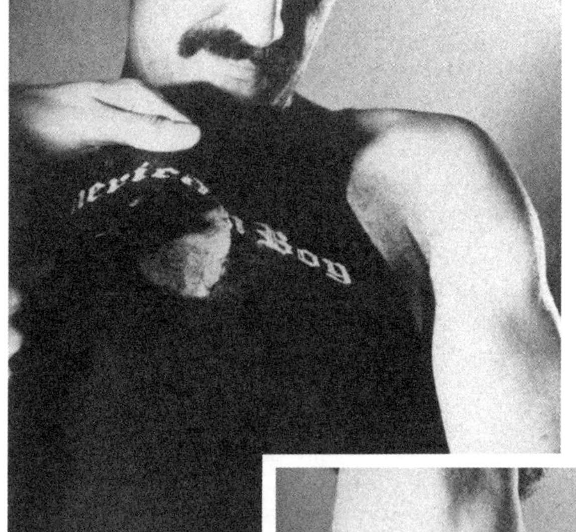

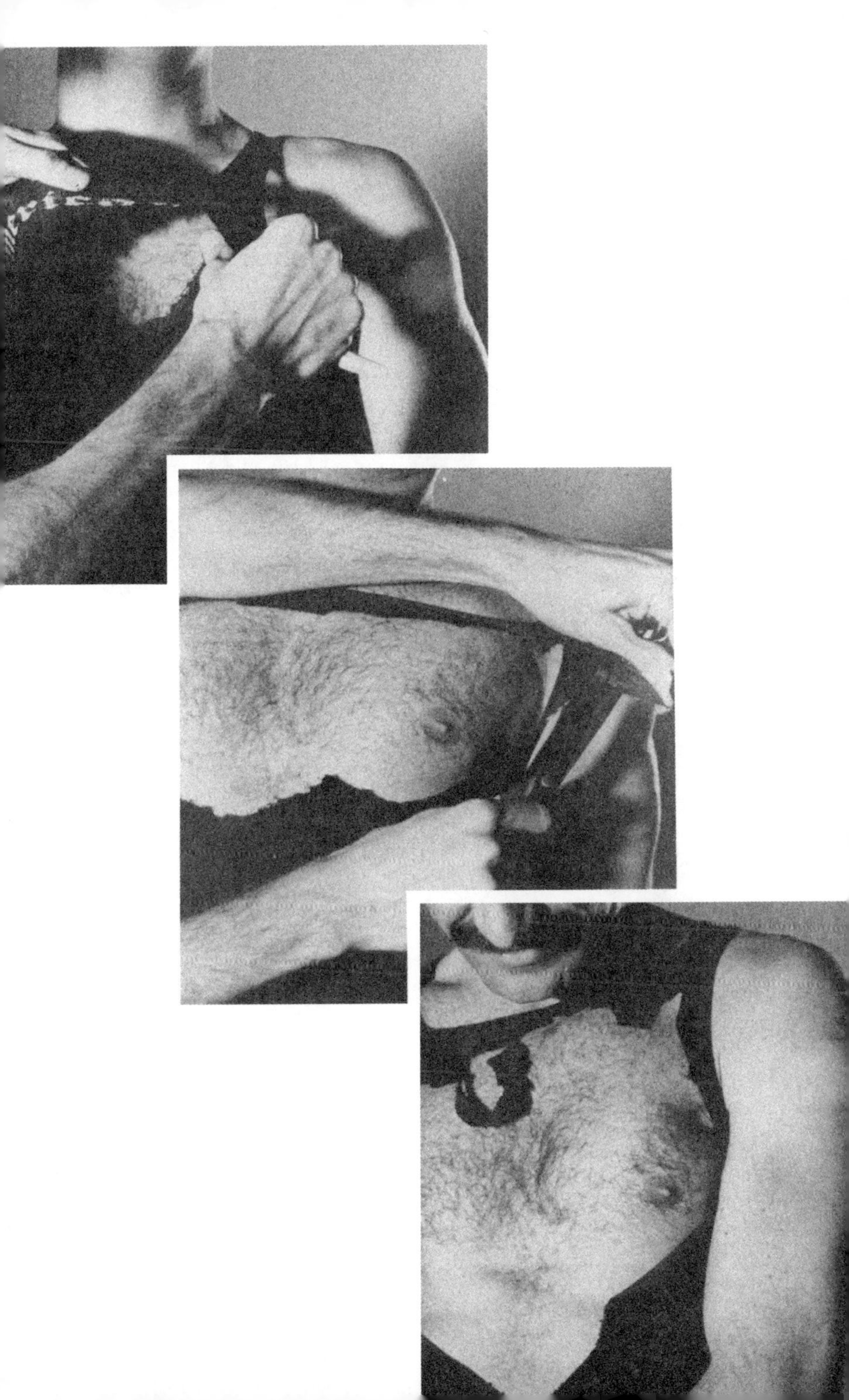

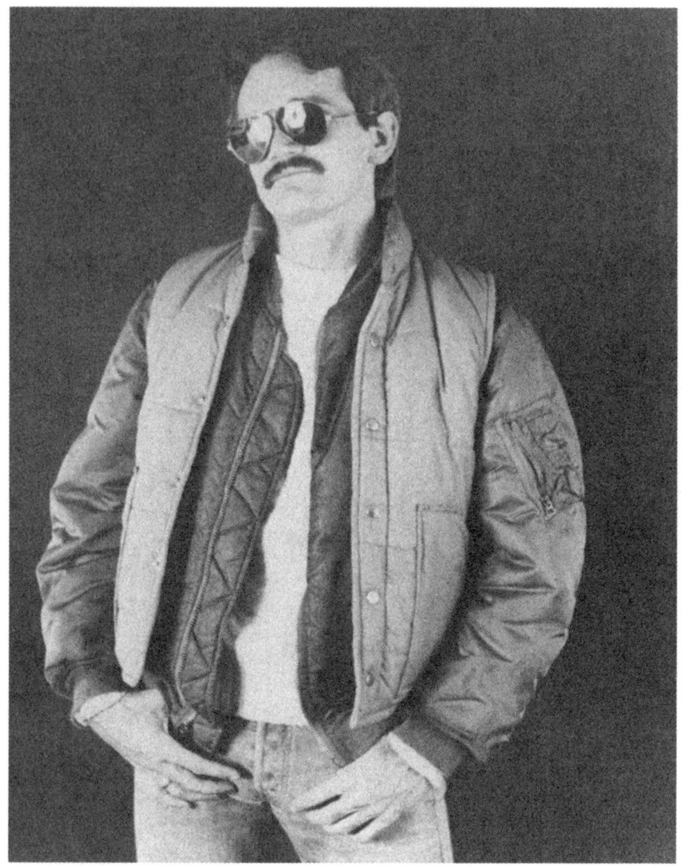

Warm, but not Hot

Coats

Butch is not fond of coats because it is very difficult to show off a well-developed set of pecs wearing a coat. Difficult, not impossible. Also, it is not particularly stunning to make an entrance dressed as the Pillsbury Dough Boy—so quilted coats are out! One Butch solution is a Levi jacket (with the sleeves ripped off) worn over a leather jacket, worn over a gray zippered sweatshirt, worn over a cotton button shirt. All the above is left unzipped or unbuttoned, and allows passersby to excavate visually through several layers of Butch's wardrobe to a terrific cleavage.

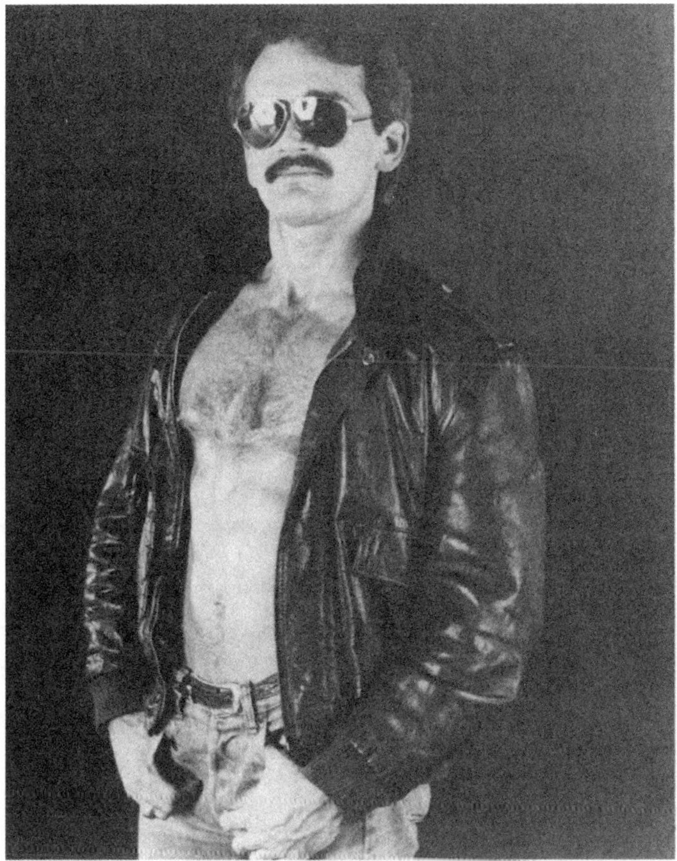

Cold, but very Hot

Another dilemma with coats is figuring out exactly what to do with them in a bar. If you check a coat, you'll never see it again. If you hold it over one arm, you'll end up looking like you're waiting for the subway. If you hold it in your lap, you'll end up looking like an old lady. If you sit on it, you'll look like you have hemorrhoids.

If you must wear a coat, remove it immediately upon entering and hang it on the head of the nearest Twinkie.

Accessories

Butch Basic is the following. Sunglasses are vital. Shirts and pants make it legal. Everything else is optional. This is a far cry from the "brilliant" dresser who spends a great deal of time gazing through the pages of *Gentleman's Quarterly*. T-shirts cost $4.50: brilliant shoes cost $240.00. Levi's cost $22.00: brilliant overcoats cost $650.00. Butch is not interested in acquiring clothing that is smarter than he is.

In buying clothes, Butch is somewhere between cheap and frugal. He will definitely be seen shopping the sales. The only reason he does not appear out of date is that his wardrobe is pared-down classic and will not go out of date until *I Love Lucy* goes out of syndication.

Underwear

Butch knows a con game when he sees one, and he is certainly not being fooled by the underwear industry. Underwear is completely unnecessary and only gets in the way. Sometimes, not often, of course, it gets in the way, in the right way.

Jockstraps. The all-time crowd pleaser. Locker-room fantasies. Fuck the team.

Jockey shorts. Beer and the boys. Fuck the fraternity.

Boxer shorts. Gentlemen in wingtips, sitting in the next stall. Fuck Wall Street.

Silk boxer shorts. Rip off silk boxers to reveal a well-muscled satin ass. Fuck Italy.

Bikinis. Leopard-skin bikini on leopard-skin seats in the back of a red Cadillac convertible with plastic Jayne on the dashboard. Fuck Hollywood.

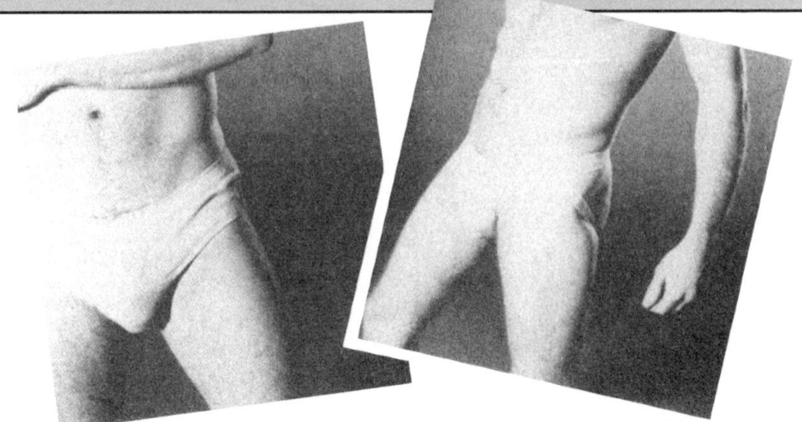

Bathing Suits

The question is not so much which swimming suit but which tan line. Butch wants a perfect tan line.

Butch will therefore wear a Speedo. The Speedo is a tight fitting, elastic suit that will never move out of place. When you take off your Speedo, you should look as though you're still wearing it. It's almost pornographic. The problem with looser suits is that they move around, producing a graduated tan line, which is unexciting. This rules out Stubbies, Dolphins, etc.

NOTE: The Speedo is dangerously close to being a bikini, and Butch is very careful to never be seen standing, let alone walking, in only a Speedo.

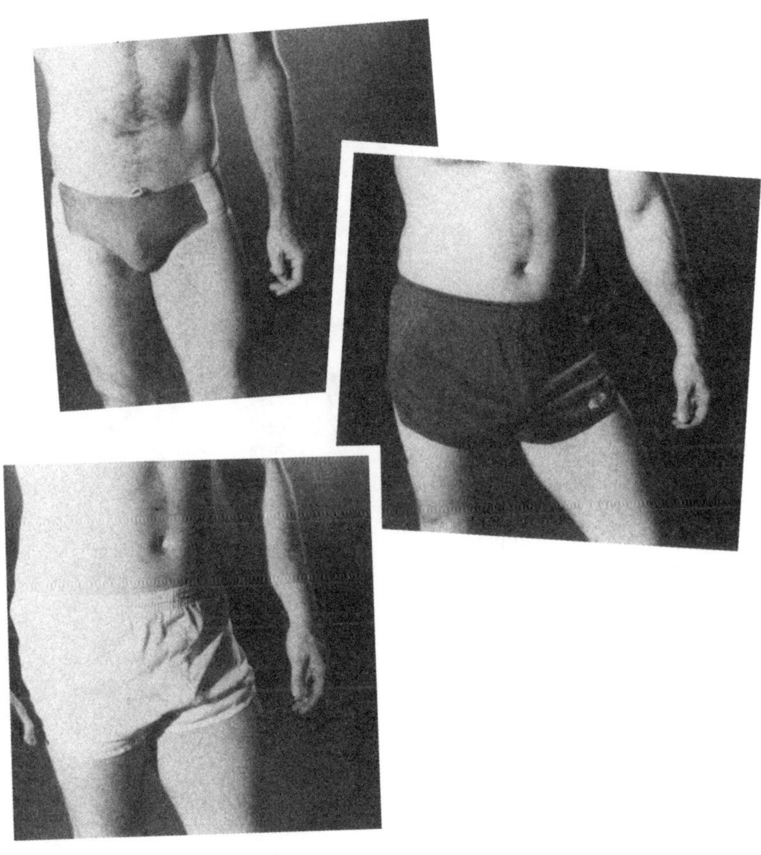

Hats

Does anyone still wear a hat?

Butch does. Peterbilt caps, yellow plastic hard hats, baseball caps, visors, ten-gallon hats, and motorcycle helmets. And no military ensemble is complete without a hat.

A sensibly sized brim casts a shadow over Butch's sunglasses, thereby doubling the air of intrigue.

A hat is always popular with the Butch who has not quite accepted the adage "Bald Is Beautiful."

Butch does not wear fedoras, Homburgs, Panama hats, or golf caps. He does not glue rhinestones on his construction hat, nor does he deplume several peacocks for his cowboy hat.

And, please, no Mousekateer ears.

Shoes

Shoes must be durable. This means military and construction shoes are extremely Butch. This also means army-surplus stores are a popular haunt for Butch. Butch will always have one pair of black shoes for late-night wear that will be equally at home in wet backrooms and park hillsides. For daytime wear, Butch will select a lighter-hued shoe. Any one of the millions of brands of athletic shoes will do fine. These can be bought anywhere. If, however, the store serves cocktails, Butch will shop elsewhere. And if Butch selects a white athletic shoe, he will immediately take a long hike on a dusty trail. Butch will *not* wear white shoes. No one should.

Fetishistic Flavors

Fetishes have always been popular with parts of the gay community. A group that is defined by a sexual term naturally feels obligated to prove itself sexual. Luckily, there are people enthusiastically devoted to this cause twenty-four hours a day, lest there still be anyone, anywhere who is still uninformed as to the meaning of the word "homosexual." These people are constantly expanding upon the concept.

Below are some of the more popular fetishes.

Uniforms. Uniforms are for people who like to play cops and robbers. Troopers, soldiers, policemen, sailors, and marines can be found

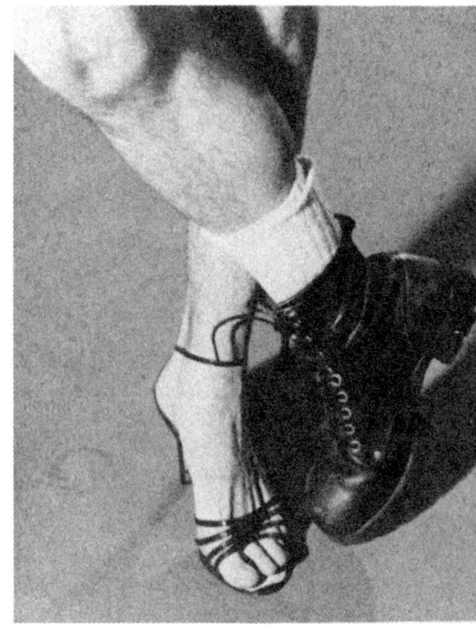

Forget matching socks, but *do* match the shoes.

executing the maneuvers in your city's more colorful neighborhoods. Besides being too strong a fashion statement for Butch, he can't afford the dry-cleaning bills. Uniforms can see a lot of action. And uniforms usually consist of several matching parts and enough medals, badges, and insignias to bring an Eagle Scout to orgasm. Not Butch, who has trouble matching his socks.

Butch will wear perhaps one item—a khaki shirt—which he'll combine with his 501s and a pair of construction boots, or tennis shoes. Or perhaps he'll wear a flight jacket and then take off the shirt and just shine his pecs.

Western. Western wear is for people who like to play cowboys and Indians. However, the shitkickers in Colorado are kicking a different kind of bullshit than those in boots in New York. Madison Avenue would have us believe that cowboys wear eel-skin boots and silk shirts.

Again, Butch will blend Western items with the rest of his wardrobe. Except for boots, which he will wear anytime he wants to feel particularly tall.

Leather. Leather is for people who like to play with...well, the latest game seems to be "hand-puppet." The leather fraternity is always the vanguard of fashion-conscious homosexuality. These gentlemen have made foreplay into a lifestyle: the world seen through leather sunglasses.

Butch has two leather accessories, a leather vest, which he wears with 50ls and usually no shirt, and chaps. He's shy about his chaps and usually wears them only in bed.

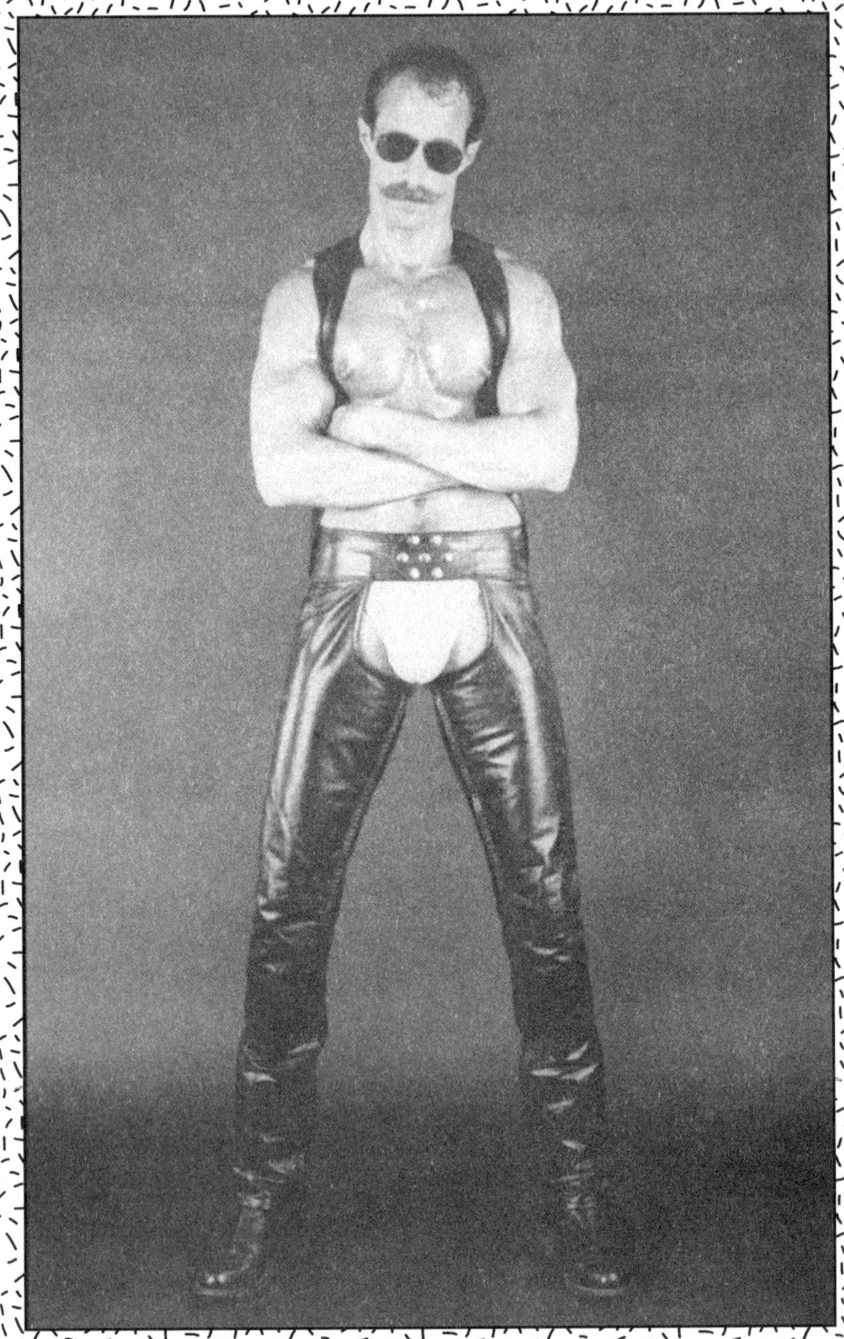

Butch Locale

The key to the Butch perspective is outdoorsy, which should in *no way* be confused with outdoors.

When the sun sets on the desert, the temperature drops fifty degrees and it is completely dark except for the bright-yellow eyes of large hostile animals. This is not a fun moment to be out for a ride. Yet riding off into the sunset is always a popular fantasy, especially when your arms are around the Lone Ranger.

Outdoorsy is a promise that the sun will never set. It is a lifestyle free of sunburn, bee stings, and poison oak. It means that in the battle between man and Nature, someone has slipped Mother Nature a Quaalude.

Butch is not interested in being outdoors. Someone else can take the purple mountains' majesty and the amber waves of grain, not to mention the herds of crickets armed with megaphones. Butch doesn't want to do it if it's on location. He is much more at home on a studio stage where the sets, the props, the temperature, the sound effects, and the lighting are all fake. Fake, yet Butch.

Therefore, Butch lives in the Big City, a place where Mother Nature has never been invited. Outdoors, with all its garish inconsistencies and gross negligence, can be easily avoided in Big Cities. The stars twinkle from their track and the sun shines on a dimmer. Butch has a green thumb for fitting outdoorsy inside.

Apartment

Butch homesteads in one of the city's colorful ghettos. At best, he lives rent-free in a decrepit, yet vaguely quaint apartment building that is slowly restoring to its turn-of-the-centry grandeur. This building has been molested by ethnic minorities for decades, and Butch's enthusiastic reconstruction has begun to resemble Dresden after the fire storms. War-zone architecture certainly enhances the ghetto, not to mention Butch's mystique.

Butch's apartment is a mess. One wall has been ripped out to locate faulty wiring. The ceiling has collapsed and is now being reinsulated. The water has been shut off ever since the toilet exploded. A stack of Masonite leans against a wall. One detects the roots of high tech.

There is no furniture. A lone mattress camps in the middle of the room. A small television perches precariously on the stack of Masonite. Several dozen beer cans have been reassigned as ashtrays. The aesthetic center of the room is a can of Crisco, placed within arms' reach of the bed.

If the idea of Butchifying your apartment with a bulldozer seems terrifying to you, there is a slightly less drastic plan. Simply repaint. Start the walls, do some of the windows, splash the doors, dribble along the trim, and then run out of paint. *Voilà*—instant Butch! Don't clean the brush, however, and do allow the roller to dry in the pan and arrange both artistically on a piece of newspaper in the window. Your apartment practically sings of sweat—with more than a hint of Abstract Expressionism.

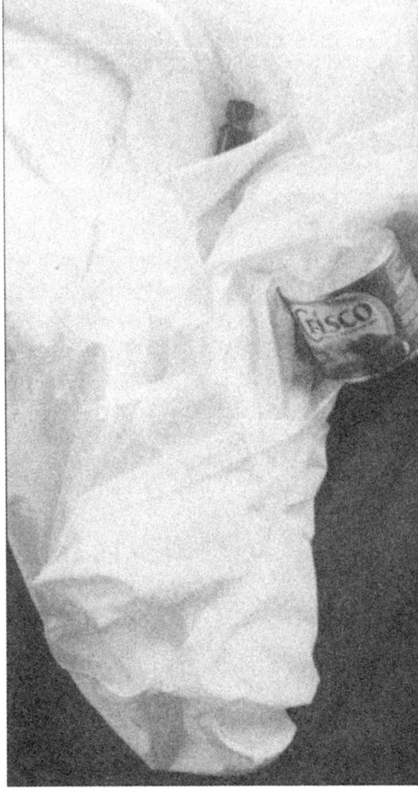

Butch Still Life #1: The Bed. Poppers on a white cloud and creamy white stuff.

The Butch Bed

The Butch bed should look lived-in. Why should Butch make his bed when he can spend the extra three minutes sleeping?

The Butch top sheet ought to be kept in a wad in the middle of the bed. A best bet is a white one with blue trim that reads "Property of Snow Sheet Rental Service" and matches the white-on-blue "YMCA" towels. The bottom sheet may be a solid-color contour that can be changed less frequently, especially if it is a color that blends with the residue of enthusiastic sex.

Decorative touches may include the Butch rustic pillow. The feathers should have long since lost their fluff, and the pillow could easily fit into a popper bottle. Butch usually can't be bothered with pillowcases.

Butch does have a blanket, but his old quilt is best kept nailed into the window, where it struggles to keep the sun out.

The Butch Refrigerator

The main purpose of the Butch refrigerator is as a place for Butch to store poppers. A jar of mayonnaise, a bottle of mustard, and a jar of crunchy peanut butter may be on the door shelf, but Butch usually cannot remember what these things are doing there. There may also be an aged ham-and-cheese sandwich that Butch picked up, along with a trick, at the Seven-Eleven on the way home from the baths several months before. The trick was favored, the sandwich forgotten.

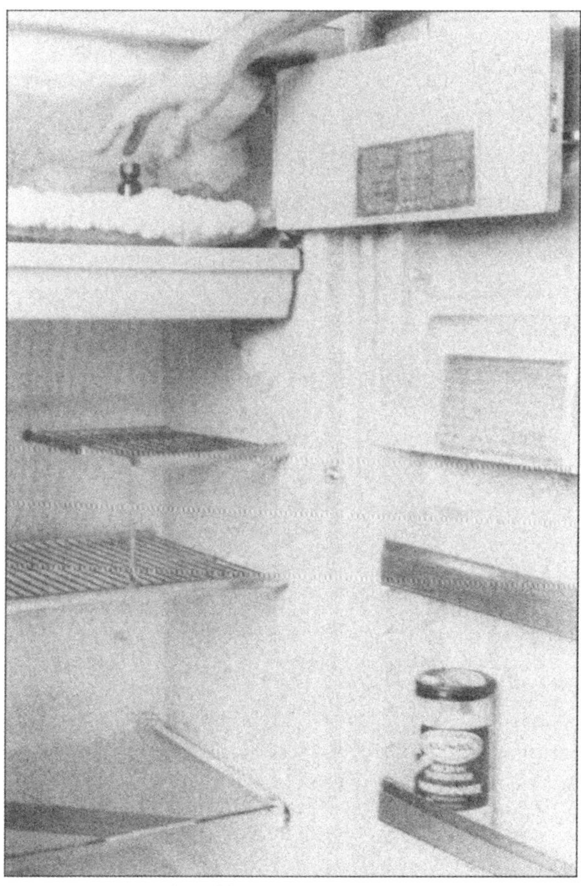

Butch Still Life #2: The Refrigerator. Poppers on a white cloud and creamy white stuff.

The Butch Diet

The Butch diet at home should be entirely liquid.

Beer. Butch drinks beer in the can because he doesn't have any glasses and he likes to crush the can in one hand.

Coffee. Butch drinks instant coffee because it is the fastest way to get the caffeine into his system.

Health drinks. The health drink is a repetitious, tiresome drink, but protein is protein and pecs are pecs.

The Butch Health Drink

Here is a basic recipe to which you may add your own Butch touches. Remember Butch would never have guava jelly or maraschino cherries to add.

ITEM	*GRAMS PROTEIN*
5 raw eggs	30.00
2 bananas	2.00
1/2 cup milk	5.00
1/2 cup juice	0.50
1/2 cup Yogurt	2.25
5 oz. protein powder	87.50
Honey to taste	——
1 Tbs. brewer's yeast	2.60
1 can tunafish	75.00
	204.85*

*Adelle Davis recommends 70 grams of protein daily for the average adult male. Thus, the remaining 134.85 grams are free to be utilized building more muscle tissue.

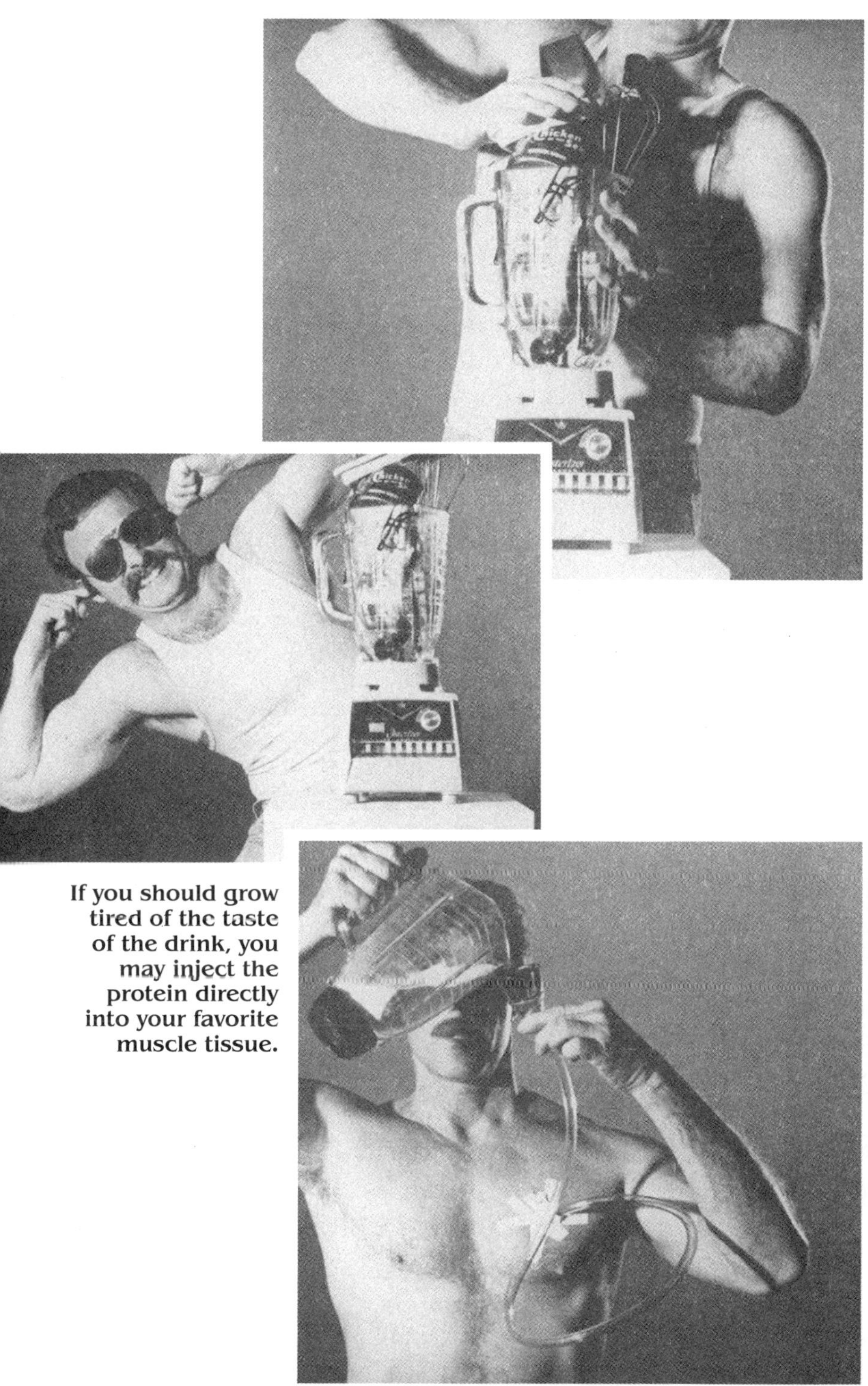

If you should grow tired of the taste of the drink, you may inject the protein directly into your favorite muscle tissue.

The Butch Bathroom

The best way to get to know a new person is by examining his bathroom. Devious tricks will race to Butch's bathroom in pursuit of articles that personify Butch's inner character. The Butch bathroom, however, is quite barren. It may take the aspiring Butch weeks to disassemble a designer bathroom in order to get it just right. Remember, the medicine cabinet should be *empty*, except for a dozen squeezed-out tubes of toothpaste and a bottle of A-200.

THE MEDICINE CABINET

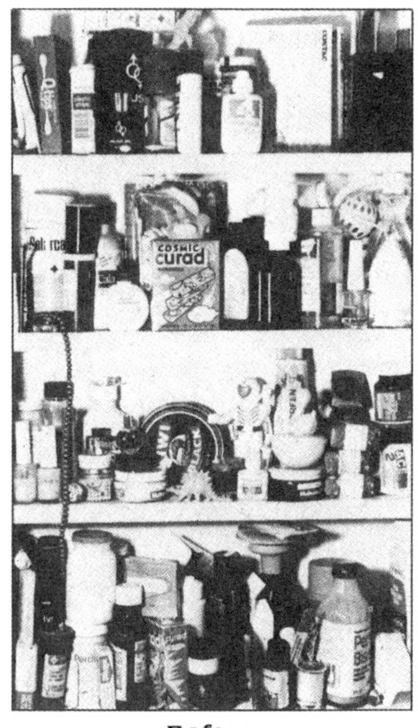

Before

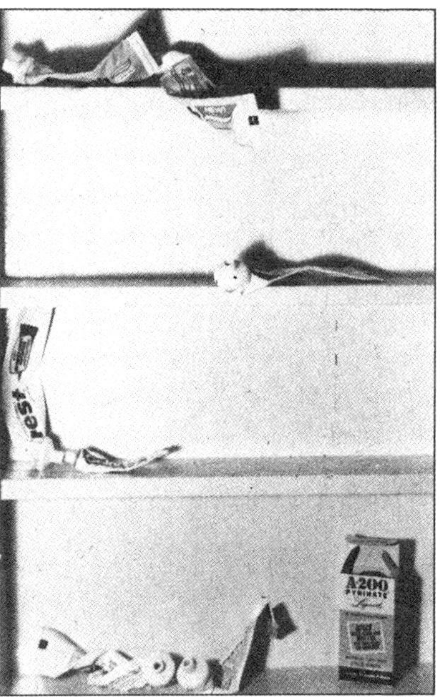

After

Things Tricks Will Not Find in Butch's Bathroom

- A soft plastic toilet seat
- Designer towels with a matching bath mat
- A shower curtain
- A douche bag hanging from the shower-curtain bar
- Framed photos of dead, female movie stars
- Framed photos of the bathroom's owner and other—unknown—homosexuals cavorting in public
- A framed joke of bathroom humor, from either *The National Lampoon* or *The New Yorker*, hanging under the light switch
- A magazine rack under the sink with *Gentleman's Quarterly*, *Interview*, *L'Uomo Vogue*, and *Architectural Digest*
- Wall-to-wall carpeting in colors that only the French can pronounce
- Exotic plants that demand special grow-lights
- Kleenex, in a designer container
- A hair-dryer, with its own special hanger
- Track lighting on dimmers
- A hand mirror, a makeup mirror, or a full-length mirror behind the bathroom door
- Pastel sculpted soap balls in a brass dish on the back of the toilet
- The top of any toothpaste tube

Butch *never* talks on the telephone while in the bathtub.

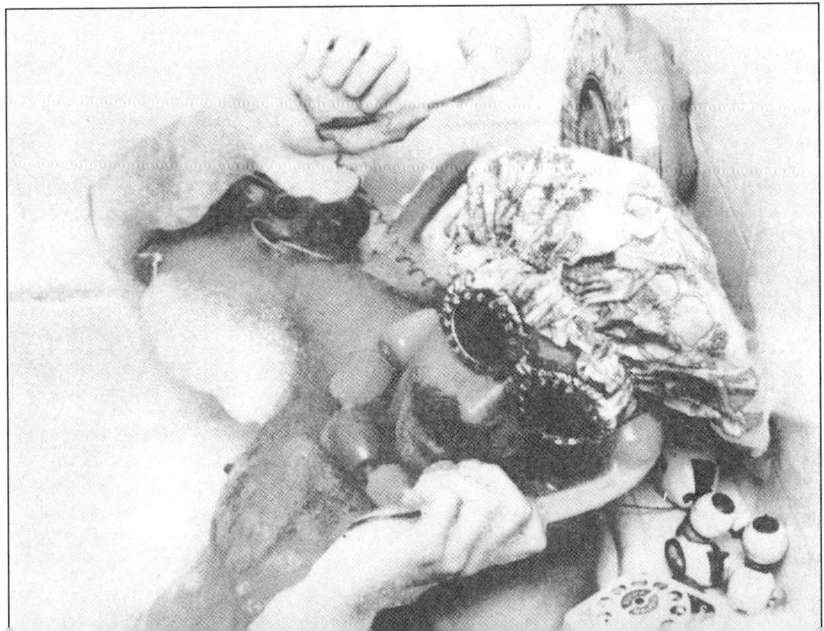

Butch Music

Butch has a tape deck and no taste. Luckily, he has a lot of friends who make tapes. Butch's idea of a great tape is one that sounds hot when he's fucking on drugs. Butch has copies of all the same tapes that they play at the baths.

Butch is *not* interested in who the latest gaggle of disco divas are.

Butch does not like Country & Western stars because all they ever sing about is getting hurt by love, which Butch cannot relate to.

Butch thinks Oldies but Goldies are for people who live in the past, which is most un-Butch.

Butch does not mind classical music because it is so boring, always a good time for a nap.

If Butch ever tires of fucking on drugs, he clicks on the clock radio and listens to whatever is on.

The Butch Closet

The Butch closet is a walk-in. Butch may sleep in his closet, which is reminiscent of the womb and always dark at nap time. The mattress barely fits into this space, just like those at the baths, and Butch *may* put up a few mirrors.

NOTE: It is sometimes difficult for some Butches to achieve orgasm in a room with fewer than two mirrors.

If Butch doesn't sleep in his closet, he may use it as a wastebasket. When Butch cleans house, he opens the closet door and throws in anything he's tired of looking at, then quickly shuts the door. When Butch finally gets around to cleaning the closet, he puts on his construction boots and jumps up and down on the heap. Should Butch feel nostalgic, he may sift through the sedimentary layers for a little archaeological dig down Memory Lane.

When Butch moves, he boxes up the entire closet and carts it off to his new closet.

The Butch Car

The Butch mode of transportation par excellence is the motorcycle.

Since not everyone has a flair for suicide, some people must resign themselves to other Butch vehicles There is no particular make of car that is *uniquely* Butch because other groups have already claimed them. Station wagons are claimed by children in carpools; as they go off to college, they get BMWs and their mothers get Volvos. White Corvettes are for men who fancy themselves as sperm. Mercedes are for people who got into real estate before 1975. Porsches are for doctors who play the options market on the side. Jeeps are for Sierra Club members. Americans who feel guilty about the economy can buy any American car built after 1979. Volkswagens are for everyone else.

It is not the make of the car but the condition of the car that certifies it as Butch. A car may be Butchified through a meticulous lack of concern for the car's condition.

How to Butchify Your Car

1. Play bumper cars. Drive into walls. Hammer dents into your fenders.
2. Smash the headlight of your choice.
3. Rip off a taillight and then tape it back with duck tape.
4. Steal your hubcaps.
5. Remove all but one of the screws holding on your license plate.
6. Break in your side vent window. Steal your radio and arrange the remaining wires in a casual bouquet. Tape cardboard over the vent window, then spray with water until the cardboard buckles and begins to leak.
7. Slash your seats and break the springs.
8. Empty several wastebaskets into the backseat along with a few orders of french fries from McDonalds.
9. Use the entire floor area as an ashtray.
10. Break off a window handle so the window is permanently stuck. Open in winter, closed in summer.

Things to Avoid with Your Car

1. Do not wash. If it rains and your car is accidentally rinsed, race to the nearest muddy road.
2. Do not decorate your dashboard or hang things from your windshield. This is best left to people who think that Christopher is still a Saint.
3. Do not keep anything useful in your glove compartment except possibly a joint, some Vaseline, a bottle of poppers, and a trick rag. Other than that, make certain that your vehicle registration is several years old, the batteries in your flashlight are older, and your maps were all charted by Magellan. The main purpose for the Butch glove compartment is to store unpaid parking tickets in.
4. Do not clean the trunk of your car. The trunk is an extension of your closet.
5. Do *not* get personalized licensed plates. If you must have plates that say "BUTCH," be certain to hang a squash blossom necklace from your rearview mirror.

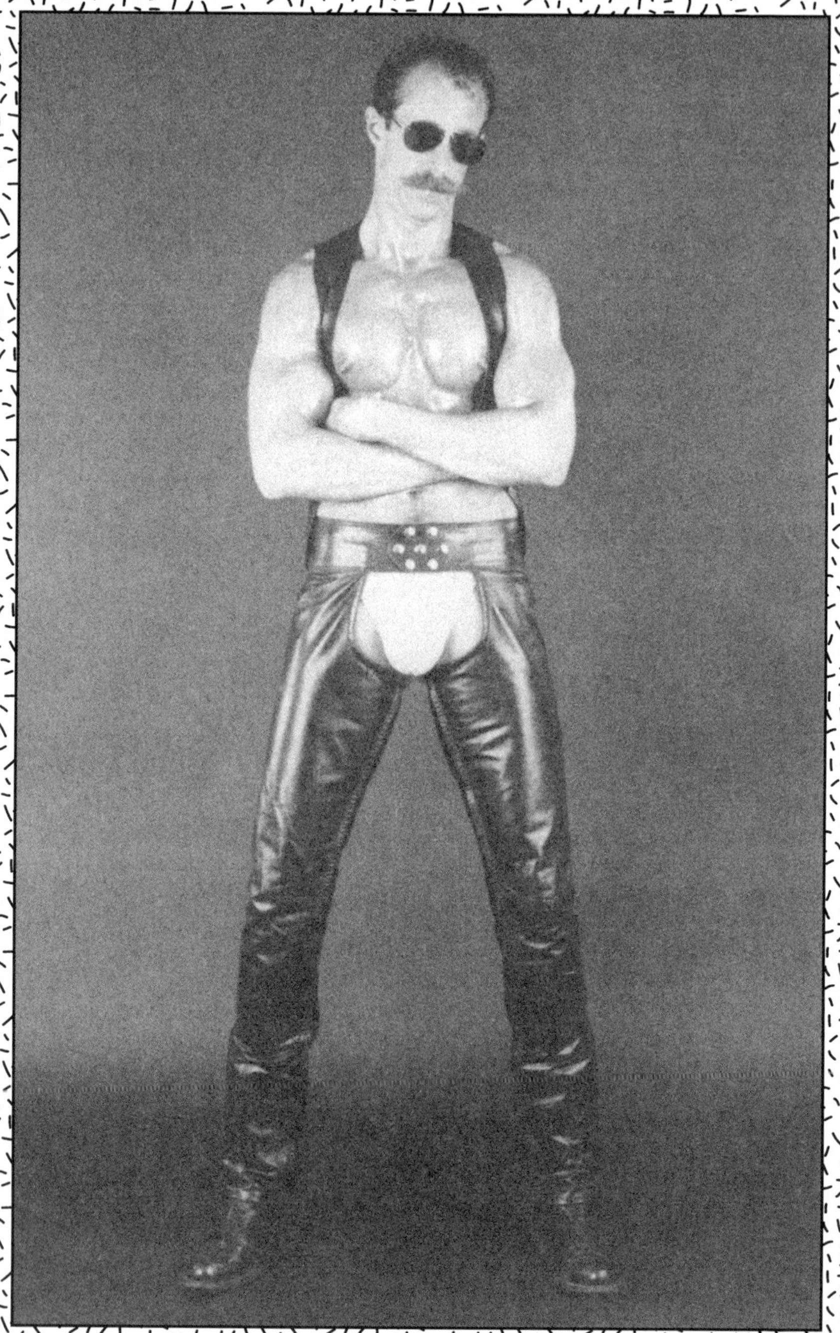

Butch Drugs

An enthusiastic use of drugs allows Butch to maintain the Butch charisma indefinitely. Drugs assure Butch that he'll never inadvertently show up anywhere on time. He'll never have to worry about where he's going because he won't remember that he was going in the first place. Drugs will help him to slouch, ensure he'll nod off for all big moments, and with drugs his socks will seldom match. No sentence will ever be completed. His car will always be on the verge of impromptu Butchification. And Butch may rest assured that he will live glare-free forever behind his sunglasses.

One minor problem with drugs is that they may freak you out. If you have not experimented with drugs, you may suddenly find yourself becoming silly, goofy, depressed, serious, spiritual, existential, or—God forbid—femme. To complicate matters, you could become quite femme, and not even care. This would be hazardously un-Butch. It is a good idea to experiment with various drugs in the privacy of your apartment before venturing out in public.

One concern people have with drugs is that they may induce incoherence and communication may become strained. Some people complain that they often can't speak, let alone converse, on drugs. These people have yet to perceive the correct mode of behavior in gay establishments. If people were supposed to talk, then bars, baths, discos, and glory holes wouldn't play their music so loud. If some ill-informed person *should* attempt to converse with you in one of these places, Butch Etiquette suggests you point out that you are wasted and wander away.

Drugs can also involve social risks. You will certainly hamper your reputation if you throw up on your friends at the disco or pass out on top of your tostada at Taco Bell. But the rewarding aspect of this is that through the magic of chemistry you can carry Butch Attitude to new depths.

Just remember one Golden Rule: Never turn down drugs. Never.

Because drugs have various effects, you may want to scan the following:

The Butch Alphabet

A. *Alcohol*, for all occasions, provides a new sense of balance. Drawback: You won't be able to remember what you did with this new sense of balance. It probably did not involve a hard-on.

B. Buff, buffer, buffering, and *Bufferin*…

C. Life as we know it would quite simply be impossible without *Caffeine*. Takes Butch from neutral to fourth gear in one death-defying cup.

D. *Dopey*, the Butch dwarf.

E. If *Elephant Tranquilizers* can knock out a two-ton elephant, imagine what they can do to Butch's mind. Drawback: While PCP increases the blood flow at a hysterical pace, the blood will bypass the brain—and the penis.

F.G.H. *Fucking Goddamn Hangover*. Shh!

I. Fill the bathtub with water and *Ice*. Add one bottle of gin. Put a straw in your mouth and climb in. Freeze off that F.G.H. in a wet martini while you take medicinal sips.

J. Butch never leaves home without at least one *Joint*.

K. The only respectable quantity of dope to buy: the *Kilo*.

L. *LSD*, amusing for figuring out which came first, sex or the universe. You can look at the person you're with and hallucinate anyone you want. Drawback: You may not be able to hallucinate a hard-on.

M. *MDA*, happy and horny, *de rigueur* at the baths. You can fantasize that you're relating to the person you're balling with. Drawback: Fantasizing your hard-on may not thrill your partner.

N. "*Nowhere* Man," a song by the Beatles.

of Fabulous Drug Abuse

O. It is possible to *Overdose on Old Wives' Tales* concerning F.G.H. cures. The only immediate, sure cure is death.

P. *Psilocybin.* Watch plants grow. Also watch plants sing and dance. Watch your body blend into the universe. Drawback: A blending penis is not a hard penis.

Q. Quick, a *Quaalude*, please! Stop that nasty trip dead in its tracks. Fall down and keep right on walking. Go to sleep and keep on talking. Drawback: Forget operating heavy machinery or hard-ons.

R. *Ripped*: the sought-after state to achieve on drugs.

S. Ms. *Snow* White is the real thing, whereas coke, which gives you a fifteen-second buzz and must be repeated forty thousand times each evening, is not.

T. People who do poppers in crowded elevators are *Tired.*

U. People who use the word "fabulous" more than a dozen times are on *Ups*. Ups are yet one more convincing reason for the legalization of euthanasia.

V. *Valium* is force-fed to people on Ups in order to make them shut up. Tranquilizes the mind for dealing with stressful situations such as the toast popping up, a waitress asking what you want, or the signal light turning green.

W. A true celebration of this list produces the ultimate Butch state: *Wasted.*

X. *X, Y and Zee*, an exceptionally indistinguishable Elizabeth Taylor film: the best nonprescription sedative available.

Y. *Yellow*, the color of your eyes if you don't sterilize your needles.

Z. Your driving pattern as described by the arresting officer.

How to Get a Hard-on (Or Tourniquet Etiquette)

When Butch is enjoying drug abuse, the situation may suddenly call for an erection. Under normal circumstances, this would be impossible. But not with the cock ring. Cock rings can be traced back to the beginnings of civilization, which says something.

In the throes of drug abuse, the circulation may slow down and blood may cease to frequent the outer appendages. Cold ears are often overlooked. Cold penises are not. By choking the base of the penis, blood is trapped in the shaft, and the resulting swollen appendage does a passable impersonation of a hard on.

There are millions of different cock-ring styles to choose from and Butch will always have a good collection to enhance any occasion.

The leather snap-on in basic black. Comes with lots of accessories like studs, spikes, ball-separators, and weights. Can be easily removed if the penis starts to suffocate.

The classic metal ring. This is difficult to remove if your dick suddenly gets a head ache. Stand on your head and have a friend stick your dick in a bowl of ice.

The leather cord. This is worn around the neck earlier in the evening. Macramé artists would envy the craftsmanship of a good C and B artist.

The rubber ring. The metal ring now comes in rubber and may be cut off in emergencies. Leaves a Butch skidmark.

Clamps, handcuffs, and other high-tech paraphernalia. Ya gotta have a gimmick.

The Seven Gates of Hell. This crowd pleaser consists of seven metal rings attached to a leather strap. It comes from the same African tribe that puts metal rings around women's necks and small frisbees in their upper lips.

The Weekend Paranoia Graph

Paranoia may raise its ugly head when one has taken too many drugs that do not go together. Ideally, the weekend should be spent partying continuously, and the drugs consumed must balance one another out. If Butch takes too many downs, he will pass out. An up will rebalance his metabolism. On the other hand, too many ups will produce hysteria, which hopefully can be doused with alcohol. Too many drugs from either the up or down families will produce excessive paranoia.

Study the following graph and observe how drugs can counterbalance each other to keep Butch in the paranoia-free zone.

Weekend Erection Possibility Chart

There are certain times when an erection is more feasible than at others. Study the following chart and maximize your possibilities.

Remember, a short waiting time between erections is generally required if an erection has been terminated by an ejaculation. This period varies in the adult male homosexual from six seconds to sixty years.

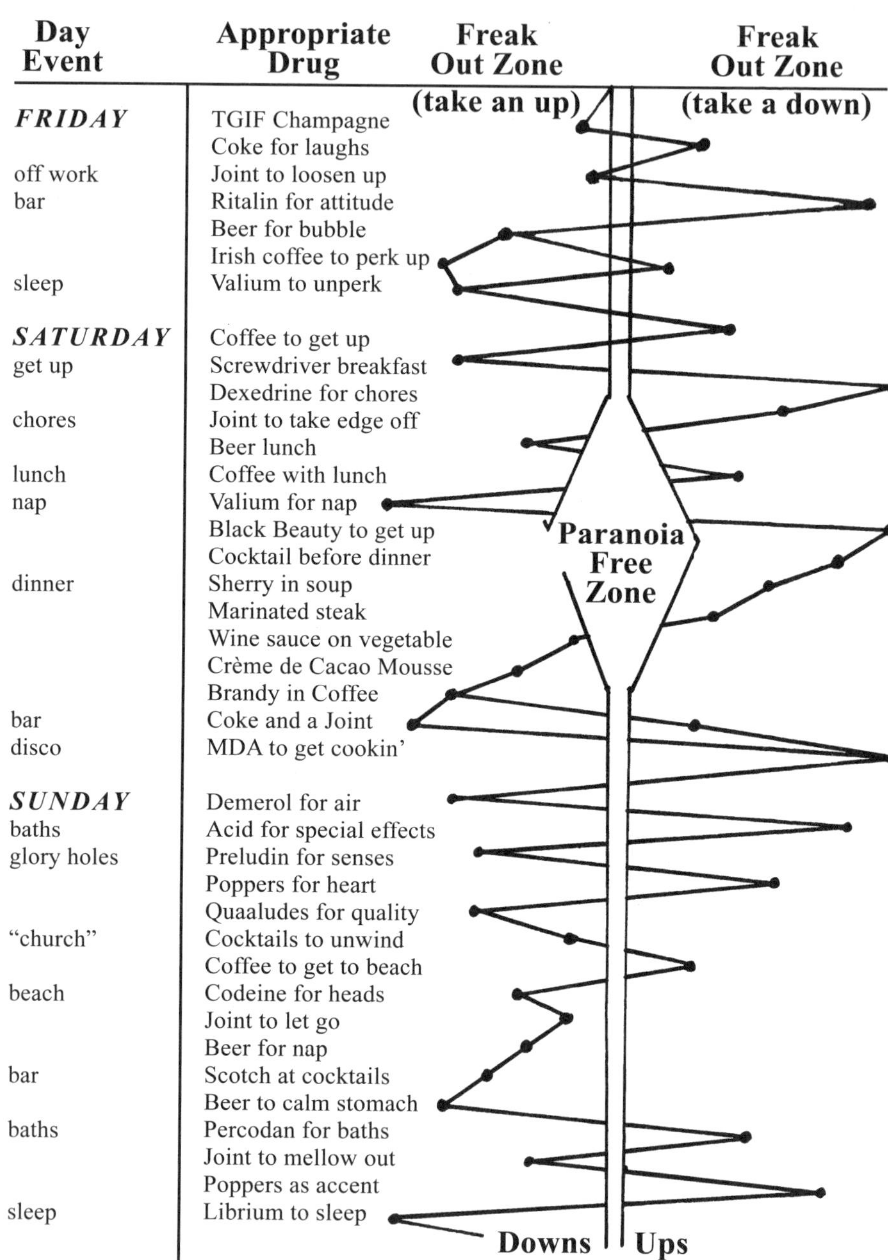

Weekend Paranoia Graph

Day Event	Appropriate Drug	Hard On	Hard Off
FRIDAY	CHAMPAGNE		
	COKE		
off work	JOINT		
bar	RITALIN		
	BEER		
	IRISH COFFEE		
sleep	VALIUM		
SATURDAY	COFFEE		
get up	SCREWDRIVER		
	DEXEDRINE		
chores	JOINT		
	BEER		
lunch	COFFEE		
nap	VALIUM		
	BLACK BEAUTY		
	COCKTAIL		
dinner	SHERRY		
	MARINATED STEAK		
	WINE SAUCE		
	CRÈME DE CACAO		
	BRANDY/COFFEE		
bar	COKE/JOINT		
disco	MDA		
SUNDAY	DEMEROL		
baths	ACID		
glory holes	PRELUDIN		
	POPPERS		
	QUAALUDES		
"church"	COCKTAILS		
	COFFEE		
beach	CODEINE		
	JOINT		
	BEER		
bar	SCOTCH		
	BEER		
baths	PERCODAN		
	JOINT		
	POPPERS		
sleep	LIBRIUM		

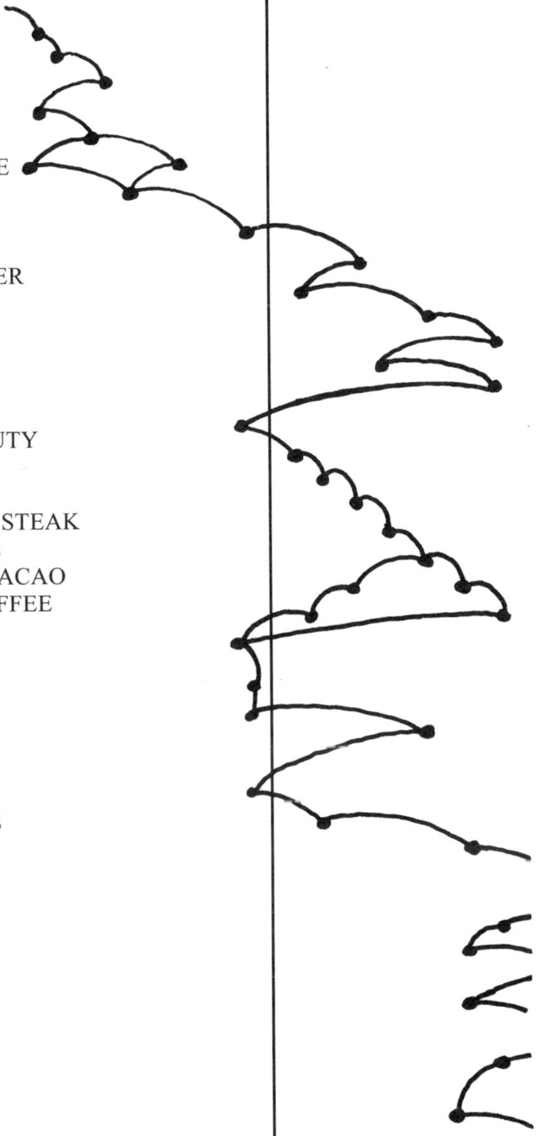

Weekend Erection Possibility Chart

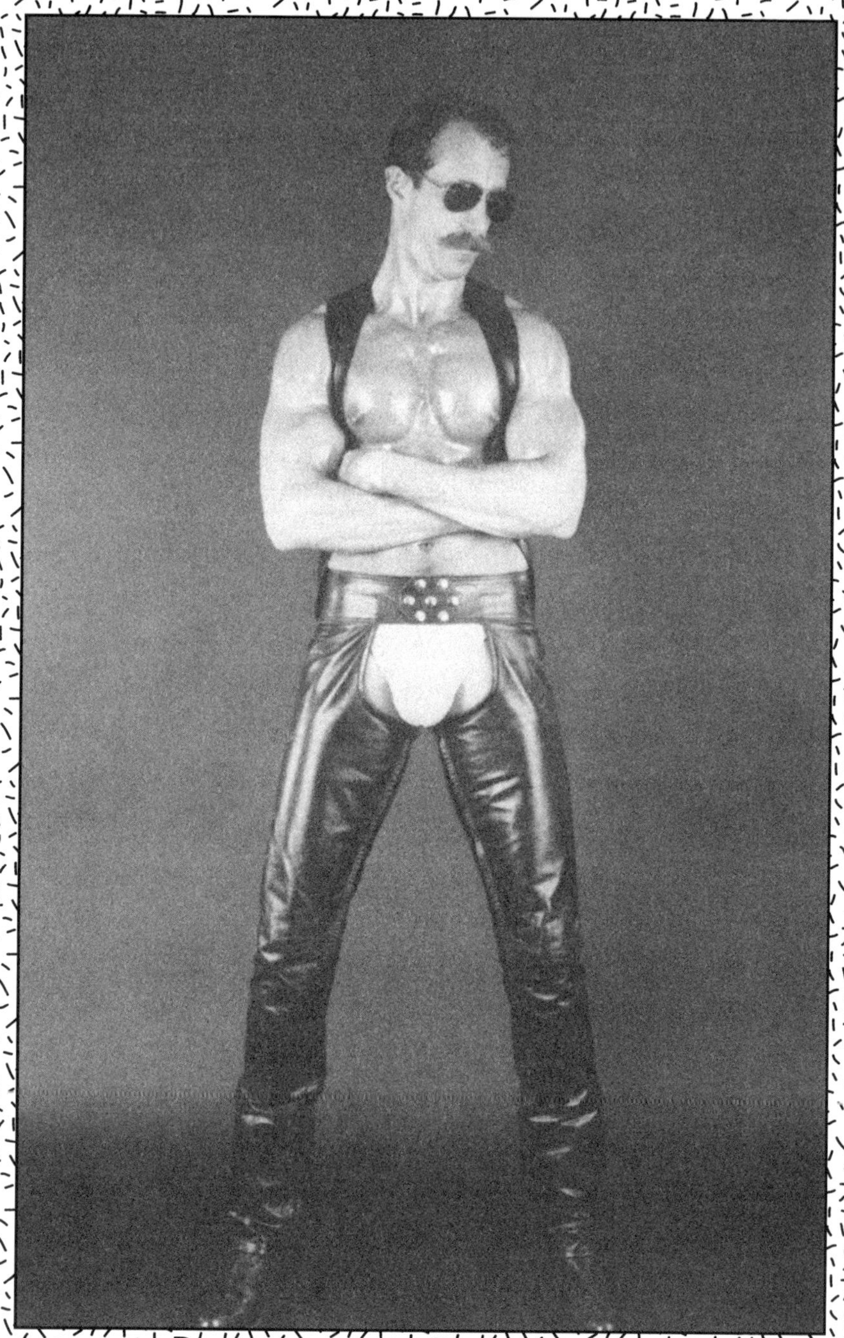

Butchopoly

Butchopoly is the game in which Butch stars. The point of the game is to get around the game board once a day. This is not so rigid as one might fear; the wild cards are always good for naps. Should you nap through most of the day, well, there's always tomorrow, and your teammates will be only too delighted to fill you in on all the gossip when you awaken.

Cheating is acceptable unless you are caught. If you don't like the roll of the dice, roll again. If you don't like your token, pick a new one. If you get tired of the game, you can always inadvertently knock the game board on the floor.

So keep those knees apart, that cleavage exposed, and those sunglasses flashing.

On your drugs?

Get ready,

Roll 'em.

Naked Breakfast

Every gay community must have at least one diner that keeps food critics working overtime thinking of derogatory ways in which to describe the food. This place serves breakfast twenty-four hours a day, but never buses the tables. The floor is wet with chlorine and the bathroom is a brothel for traveling parasites. The bathroom, however, is also permanently out of order. It is a decorative feature required by law.

It is in this diner that the Butch breakfast is eternally served, combining the two elements that raise the meal to the plateau of Communion: Mom and Man. The 1950s sitcoms defined Mom as the All-American Archangel she should have been. The Mom who only went into the bedrooms to change the beds and never went into the bathroom at all. The Mom who spent all her time in the kitchen continuously baking brownies, squeezing orange juice, and making lots of extra bacon. She was always in a good mood and you were never expected to tip. The Butch diner has one waitress, either a very old woman or a very old queen, and she does a spectacular imitation of Mom. Her total purpose in life is to wait on Men: Men at mess, at mining camp, boot camp, lumber camp, even summer camp. There's no place like Home Sweet Home on the range.

There's nothing quite so wonderful in the Big City as walking into a diner and having the waitress greet you by name and ask if you want the regular. Of course you do, and even though it may be more complicated than *Finnegan's Wake*, she jots it all down without asking you a single question. Mom loves you 'cause you're special and you don't mind leaving her a tip.

Besides being covered with dirty dishes, the tables are also covered with newspapers. Butch likes to glance at the paper while he eats.

A Sample Butch Menu

3 Scrambled Eggs, slightly moist. Butch is the only person in the U.S. not concerned with cholesterol, and could not even pronounce arteriosclerosis. He contentedly ingests a dozen eggs a day.

4 Strips of Bacon. Butch feels bacon is traditional in spite of the dangerous preservatives that have been added.

Toast. Butch wants whole wheat, never white, rye, or nelly cinnamon.

Strawberry Jam. Marmalade is too pushy and Mixed Fruit is too boring.

Large Orange Juice. Anita Who?

Substitutions. French Fries for Hash Browns. Hash Browns are the disintegrating remains of last night's baked potatoes dressed up with green and red peppers. Yeck!

Side Order 1. A medium-rare hamburger patty dripping with A-1. No meal is complete without at least one hamburger.

Side Order 2. Three pancakes, with extra butter and honey. Butch loves carbohydrates and anything that even mildly resembles a dessert.

Water. Two glasses, one without ice so Butch can take his handfuls of vitamins, and the other with, so Butch has some ice to chew on at the end of the meal.

Coffee. Butch's cup should never be more than a few sips from the top. There should be plenty of sugar and cream on the table.

You may take off your sunglasses, but it is not necessary. Remember, you can always hide behind the paper. Because everyone is a regular, you may nod at people. You can feel quite popular by the time you pay your bill. No fair cruising, though; some people don't have on their sunglasses.

A Few Added Hints on Food

Butch eats all meals out. He eats whenever he feels hungry. His priorities in choosing restaurants are: "Is it cheap?" followed by "How far is it from here?" Butch thinks gourmet is a has-been crooner.

A few points to remember.

- Always insist on French's mustard. Never settle for French crap like Dijon.
- Never order Roquefort dressing. People who want to pay seventy-five cents extra for salad dressing are social climbing. Never order the house dressing. Aside from being patronizing, you will end up with lettuce covered with yogurt, honey, or Shake 'n Bake. The correct choice is Thousand Island, a fifty-fifty blend of catsup and mayonnaise.
- French fries go with everything, especially ice-cream sundaes.
- Mayonnaise is the perfect lubricant for anything that is too dry.
- Parsley is not to be eaten. It is to be played with.
- If a menu is too expensive, tell the waitress that you just ate and ask her what kind of pie they have.
- If the menu is written in a foreign language, leave immediately.

Brunch

Butch would not be caught dead at Brunch.

If you land on this square, you must go directly to jail. You may not collect $200. Perhaps you should try another game. Like Old Maid.

Having finished his fourth gallon of coffee at breakfast, Butch heads for the nearest gay beach. This step is imperative—Body Maintenance, Part One: The Incredible Tan line.

Baby-oil Oasis (Or Butch at the Beach)

When tanning clinics perfect the four-star tan Butch will no longer have to put up with the insane lighting (broad daylight) available at the beach.

Butch arrives wearing cutoffs, the world's darkest sunglasses, and his Butch day pack. He does not have a lounge chair, an umbrella, pillows, rubber rafts, a Styrofoam cooler, a picnic basket, or a fat female friend in a two-piece suit who knows all the boys on the beach.

As the gay community likes being crowded, even on an enormous beach it will cluster into a tight formation. Butch slowly trudges toward the center of the group, meticulously scanning the area for the ideal spot to encamp. He especially wants to avoid sitting next to portable televisions, silver ice buckets, Carmen Miranda beach hats, and children of all ages. Butch usually approaches the Butch corps, easily discovered lying in formation in the center of the beach. As their heads slowly pivot, Butch can see himself reflected in dozens of mirrored sunglasses.

Butch disrobes with drill-like precision, undressing and setting up shop in a series of artistic maneuvers. Butch anoints his entire body with several different kinds of oils and lotions, depending upon how prone an area may be to acne. Ideally, the oil is to be applied sensuously so as to raise the temperature of the beach another ten degrees.

After Butch has baked in the sun awhile, he will promenade down by the waves. Remember, *do not stand* in your Speedo, pull on your cutoffs before standing up. Should you be in an extremely whimsical mood, you may wear a silky pair of Dolphins, but this is only to the edge of the water, *not* to the food stand.

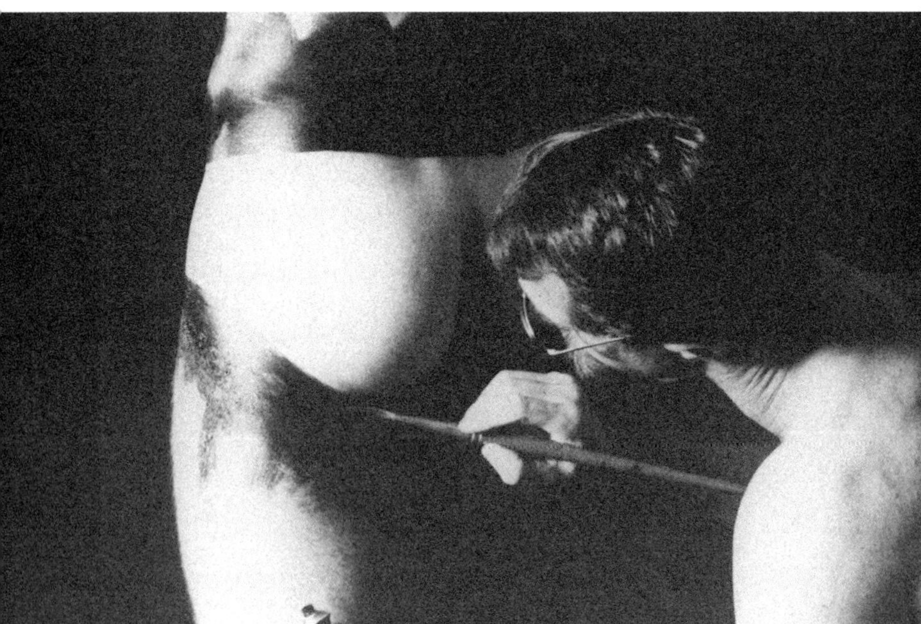

A tan line should look painted on.

How to Disrobe at the Beach

Butch haiku: Imagine Lawrence of Arabia performing the Japanese Tea Ceremony.

1. Unfold bedspread, shake several times, and let flutter to the sand. The bedspread should be faded and have seen all the major gay beaches. Tuck all four edges into the sand
2. Toss day pack in the upper center of the bedspread
3. Remove towel, shake, lower to center of bedspread. The towel does *not* advertise Broadway shows or what you do in bed. Leave the advertising to your body.
4. Still standing, lift one foot and remove shoe and sock then do second foot. Because falling over is a high risk, you are demonstrating breathtaking Butch balance.
5. Sit on lower end of towel. Slide shorts off.
6. You are now in position for oil-up.
   a. Rub baby oil on your chest, slowly massage pecs.
   b. Squirt more oil on your abs, slather the area.
   c. Knead the remaining oil into the biceps.
   d. Squeeze lotion on the forearms, the shoulders, the back, and the face.
   e. Gently apply sun screen to sunburnt areas.
   f. Forget the legs.
7. Slide backward and gently rest your head on your day pack. Take a deep breath. Think Tan.

This step is the Second Round of Body Maintenance. After all, what good is a Saint-Tropez tan if it's not showcased on overdeveloped muscles?

Walking along the beach can be a fun time for Butch to feel popular as he casually nods to everyone. In truth, no one recognizes anyone else because this is the only moment of broad daylight in a lifetime of dark hallways. Pretend you've been intimate with people and they'll wave back. Promenading the shoreline is also a good time to find out who is selling which drugs, who is giving the upcoming parties, which gyms are hot, and which stores are having sales. Assure yourself of an invitation to an upcoming party by complimenting the upcoming host on his hot tan.

Remember: DO *not* put your hands on your hips, do *not* talk with your hands, and do *not* get into the water. Butch is too lazy to bother putting oils and lotions on twice.

If Butch does venture to the snack bar, he may slip on a tank top if his nipples are recovering from a long night out. He may also slip on a pair of shoes if he can't march stoically the entire way. At no time will Butch dart from towel to towel, screeching obscenities.

Butch leaves the beach five minutes ahead of the crowd. This gesture says, "Sorry, I gotta run, but I've got a million parties to get to." Actually, Butch is going home to take a nap before deciding which bar to stop at on his way to the tubs.

Sweet Sweat (Or Butch at the Gym)

Tits are in, the bigger the better. Women, who until recently have been the only humans with tits, used to complain, "Fuck it, men only want me for my body." Butch wants to be wanted for his body. He likes being a sex symbol.

Going to the gym is not something Butch looks forward to. He can think of millions of things he would rather be doing, such as taking a nap. But Butch has also developed a heightened sense of his musculature, and if he misses even one workout, he can immediately detect atrophying muscles. Butch has been spotted escaping from hospitals dragging his I.V. bottle with him down the street as he searches out the nearest gym. This is Butch's commitment in life, and he will arrive at the gym in spite of fever, nausea, and crippling hangovers.

This does not make going to the gym any easier. So Butch will procrastinate as long as possible. Thus he will enter the gym feeling exhausted and trudge to the locker room feeling depressed, while every person he passes points out that he is late.

NOTE: There are two rows of lockers in the locker room, upper and lower. Butch always insists on the upper. He is not interested in bending over.

First Butch weighs himself. This elicits a gasp, a shudder. Everyone in the locker room looks up and inquires, "Butch, what's the matter?" Butch points to the scale. He has lost a quarter of a pound. The locker room choruses, "Don't worry, Butch, you still look great! You'll gain it back." Butch sighs as a ray of hope tweaks his left nipple. And the chorus continues, "And you still have the best pecs in town." Butch then feels relieved enough to begin his workout.

There are two parts to a workout. One is the actual workout, the second is eavesdropping on all the gossip. This is a good time for Butch to find out who is selling which drugs, who is giving the upcoming parties, which bars are hot, and which stores are having sales. Should someone be giving an upcoming party, make certain that you are invited by remarking how much larger his tits are.

Butch grinds through his workout sweating profusely. If you don't sweat, visit the water fountain between sets and splash yourself.

Butch often likes to look in the mirror and flex various muscles. This may inhibit the beginner, who's been avoiding mirrors all his life.

Butch never makes loud noises while working out. This is considered a cheap attention-getting device. This is no time to talk dirty.

Butch works out alone, but he will not hesitate to ask someone to spot for him. Nobody ever will want to, but who is to say that Butch is not giving an upcoming party...

A SPECIAL NOTE: If you want to see what Butch looks like when he ejaculates, watch his expression as he does the last rep on his last set of bench presses.

The Butch Gym Outfit

Jockstrap. Finally! An athletic supporter for a somewhat athletic event.

Gym Shorts. All cotton, faded, torn. These shorts ought to have worked out in the best gyms, the major beaches, and more than one bathhouse.

Socks. White, possibly with stripes. Stripes should not match.

Shoes. White or black leather tennis shoes, dirty enough that they look beige. Shoes should match.

Tank top or T-shirt. Should be filled with holes and advertise a university you never went to or a famous heterosexual gym. Shirt is taken off after you warm up or if you see someone you want to flirt with.

Sweatpants. These are popular only with people who have extremely skinny legs.

Leather belt. This is worn ostensibly to save the back in heavy lifting. Actually, it keeps the midriff and love handles tucked in.

Leather gloves. These are worn ostensibly to allow a firmer grip on heavy weights. Actually, they keep hands soft for jacking

Head bands. These are ostensibly worn to keep sweat from running down the face. They're actually worn because they're the latest fashion fad. Forget 'em.

If Butch ever approaches a state resembling an emotional reaction, it will occur at the end of his workout. He may possibly sing in the shower. And as he dresses, he may even chide all the newcomers for being late.

More important than all this, however, is fashion. What can be worn at the gym to remain totally Butch? See page 91.

How to Avoid Sharing Equipment

Butch likes to work out alone and does not want to share equipment. Some people will try to meet Butch by asking if they can work out with him. This is tacky and Butch will respond accordingly:

- No, you may not.
- I'm on my last set.
- I'm doing my sets too close together.
- Did you just start working out?
- You should use lighter weights and try for definition.
- You should use heavier weights and try for bulk.
- You should try steroids.
- You should try developing your personality.
- Go away.

The next step in Butchopoly is a Wild Card. Butch may choose to nap through it.

Cocktail Coward (Or Butch at Cocktails)

The cocktail party was invented by Noël Coward so he could have a built-in audience while he leaned on his mantelpiece, sipped dry gin martinis, and tried out new material for his next play. (The play would be about people leaning on mantelpieces, sipping martinis, and saying dreadfully dishy things about each other.)

It is unfortunate that the cocktail party did not die when Noël did. Tuxedos with martinis still reunite around the mantel from six to eightish each evening. The Brie quiche is cut, the hunky butler is coked, the poodles have been slipped their doggie downers, and the Tyd-y-Bowl is working overtime.

But something is awry. The designer dish has suddenly crash-landed in the California Dip. The word "dreadfully" has been pushed once too often unto the breach. The tuxedos are on the verge of terminal ennui. Can *anything* save this affair?

Enter Butch. Butch is never invited to cocktail parties; he is always dragged along by one of the guests who promises him they won't stay more than a second. The tuxedos bristle as Butch enters in his Butch glory: the dusty tennis shoes, the grass stains on the knees of the faded 501s, that loaded basket yearning to breathe free, the sweat stains in the armpits, the missing buttons revealing two bronzed pectorals, and—with a twist of the head two divine nipples. The gaggle of tuxedos, heads all tilted to one side, collectively gasp.

The Games commence. Butch coolly eyes the tuxedos as he wanders to the window to look down on the city. The butler brings him a beer. Butch's date wanders around the room collecting accolades for having discovered Butch. The guests have spent a lifetime sublimating sensuality into arrogance, and the group sum of suppressed lust is about to blast Butch out the window. One by one, the guests wander up to Butch to inform him of their net worth in real estate. Butch crushes his beer can and drops it on the butler's tray.

"Would you care for another?" the butler asks.

"Wanna fuck?" Butch asks.

They climb the stairway to heaven and disappear into the master bedroom. The living room bubbles in turmoil. The hosts panic. Butch's date pops a dozen Valium. The gossip accelerates as all eyes remain glued to the staircase. Everyone still finds time to wander by Butch's date and offer a pleasant, "So, dear, do you have plans for the weekend?" Should Butch's date live so long, he will definitely be leaving town over the weekend.

Butch leaves the bedroom first. He looks more relaxed. He saunters down the stairs, gets himself a new beer, and plops down on the sofa.

The butler wanders out of the bathroom. His eyes are crossed and he is grinning from ear to ear. He walks into the wall, bounces backward, and falls down the stairs. He gets up and wanders out the front door, never to be seen again.

All the guests join Butch on the sofa. Butch's date drags him onto the terrace. The date screams, he threatens, he breaks down and cries. Butch is unamused. He calls a cab and goes to the baths. Butch's date cries himself to sleep on the chaise.

Noël would have loved it.

The next step in Butchopoly is not optional and may not be napped through.

The Posing Olympics (Or Butch at the Bars)

There exists a group of people who enjoy talking about how Tired the bars are. These people stand around bars getting depressed as they watch other

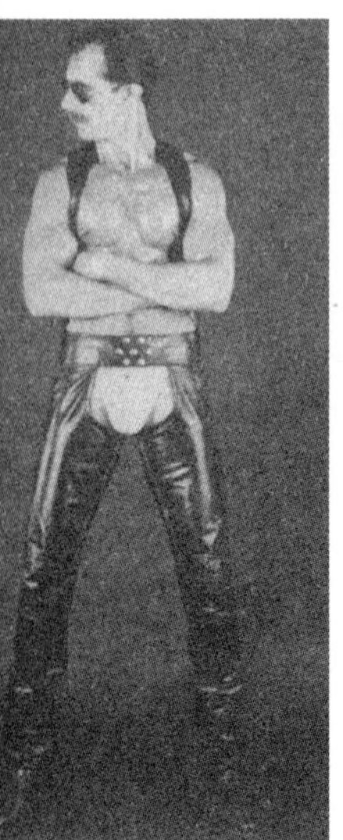 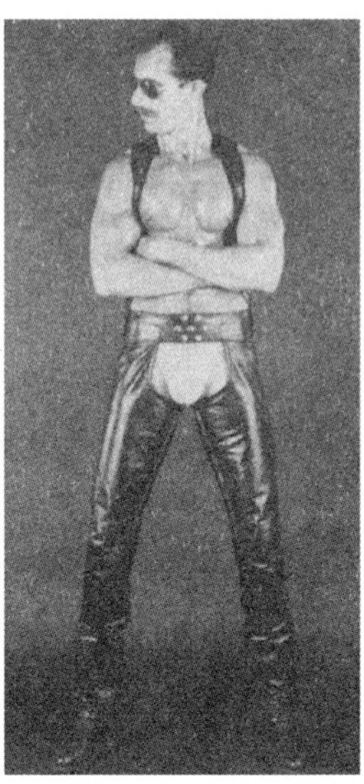 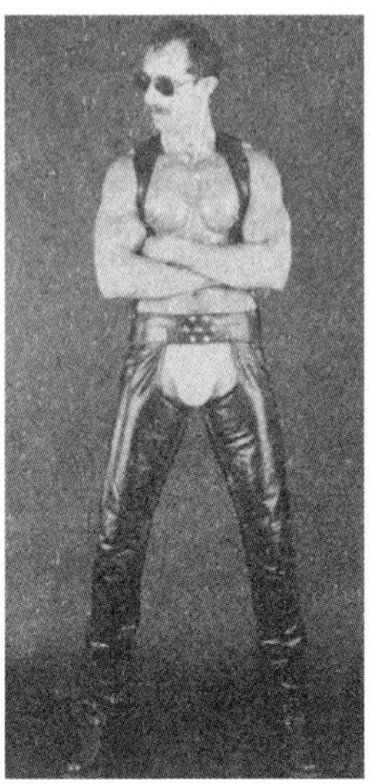 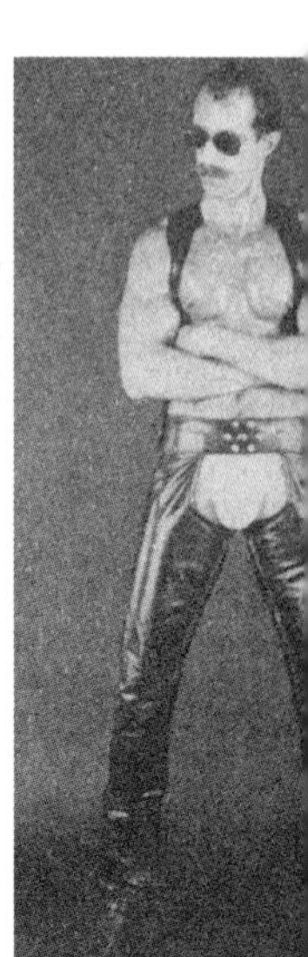

POSING AS ART: Minimal expressionism vibrates in the existential simplicity of a pure Zen brushstroke.

people feel Up. And they get more depressed as the people feeling Up feel up other people feeling Up, and often leave the bar together. Bars are not Tired; watching other people score is Tired; and these people have yet to realize the main purpose of bars.

Bar owners are not stupid. If everyone scored in a bar, the place would be empty. So bars have been designed as places where people can gently come onto their drugs, get acclimated to altered states, and then head off to the disco to shake it up.

Therefore, bars resemble large isolation tanks. The darkness is padded with billows of smoke and encased in a wall of sound. Bars are a great place to be alone. And should the experience become too primal, bars conveniently serve alcohol—everyone's favorite, nonprescription tranquilizer.

It is rude to go into a bar feeling depressed. After all, other people have taken their time and their drugs to feel Up. To arrive at a bar feeling Up, just remember that the last crabs visiting your apartment (groin/crotch/armpits) are finally dead. Recall that last night's cranberry juice took care of that burning; so it must have been NSU after all. Think back on those weird bumps that went away all on their own. Also recall that your bowels are back to normal—probably too much coffee again. God's in His Heaven, all's right with the world.

Enter the bar slowly. You are Gary Cooper. Your eyes scan the bar looking for someone to shoot. The bar freezes, drinks poised in midair,

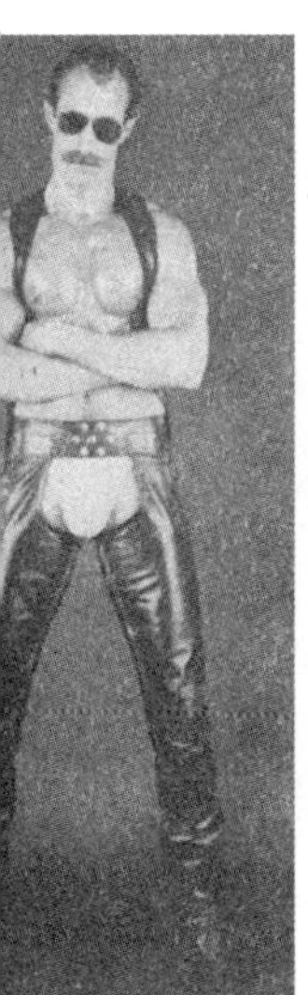
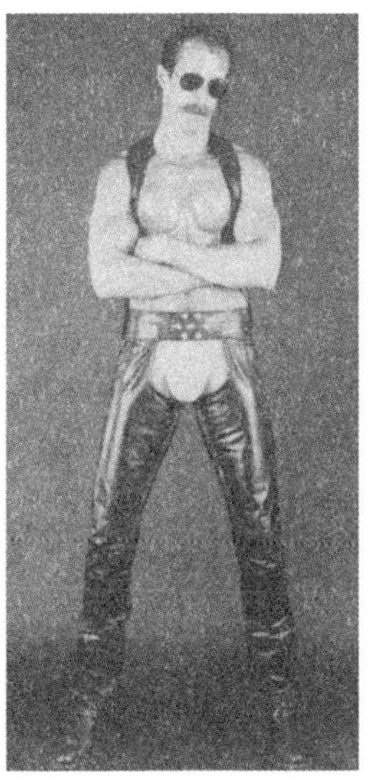
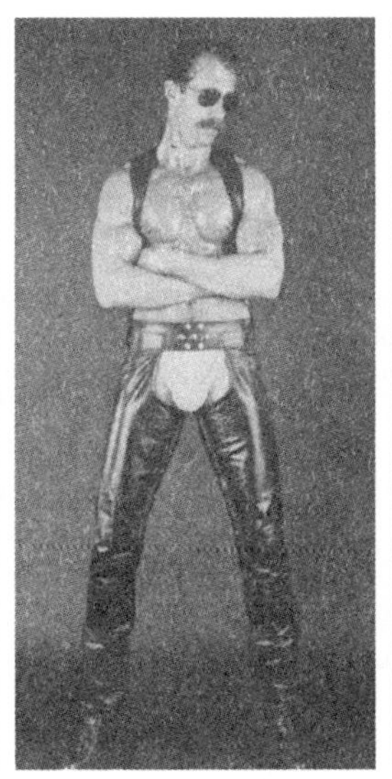
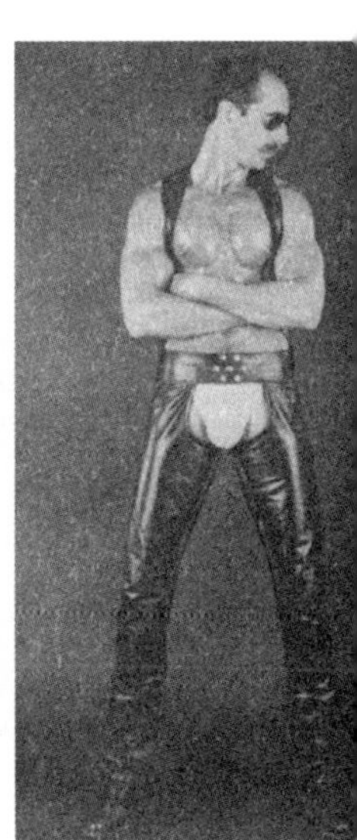

pinkies reaching for the ceiling. Slowly walk through the bar, disappear into the bathroom, and relieve yourself.

The Butch crowd dominates the center of the bar. This is a good spot for Butch to find out who's got drugs, who's having parties, which discos are hot, and any stores that may be having sales. If someone is giving a party, be sure to act interested in whatever he's saying to ensure yourself an invitation. One fun thing about bars is that you have to lean over and talk directly into someone's ear to be heard over the loud music. This looks secretive and helps establish your reputation for being in-the-know.

After a while, Butch will move into uncharted waters. He will find a relatively unpopulated corner of the bar and begin Posing. Posing is the most popular pastime in bars and Posing aficionados will soon surround Butch and stare in approval. Occasionally, two well-known Butches will get together for a Pose-off, always a crowd-pleaser.

After an exhausting set of bar Poses, Butch may go take a leak. Bars are not designed for flow. The gay community likes to fill up bars the same way that fraternities used to like to fill up phone booths and small foreign cars in the 50s. A sign over the door will proclaim "Occupancy 216." This means 216 thousand. The only way to get anywhere in a bar is to press away from the wall and get into the flow. The flow is usually going to the bathroom.

This flow design is not without merit. Should you see someone you want to pursue, it is considered desperate to go over and say "Hi." Instead, go to the bathroom, then return to your original posing spot. Of course it will be taken. Act pissed-off and scout around for a new location, which will turn out to be right next to your potential new conquest.

Do not go home with anyone from a bar. You never know. What if you get them home and they can only come to the sound of ripping silk panties?

Stamping Out Smile Buttons

Unfortunately, there are some naive Twinkies out there who are too young to show respect for their elders, much less awe or terror. Because these kids are too young to stay up late with the big kids, they take their drugs way too early and peak at the most inopportune moments. These Divas of Premature Emancipation will arrive at the bar ripped to the tits and proceed to run around shrieking, "Party! Party!" which does not particularly endear them to the rest of the clientele.

When a Twinkie focuses his vision on Butch, he will immediately mistake Butch's concentration for depression. He'll race right over to cheer Butch up and inadvertently destroy a carefully worked out set of Poses. Twinkie will shout, "Smile!"

The Butchest thing to do is not react to this bullshit. Alas, Twinkies will take this as a sign that they will have to work harder to get you to smile. Your Butch response will be, in order:

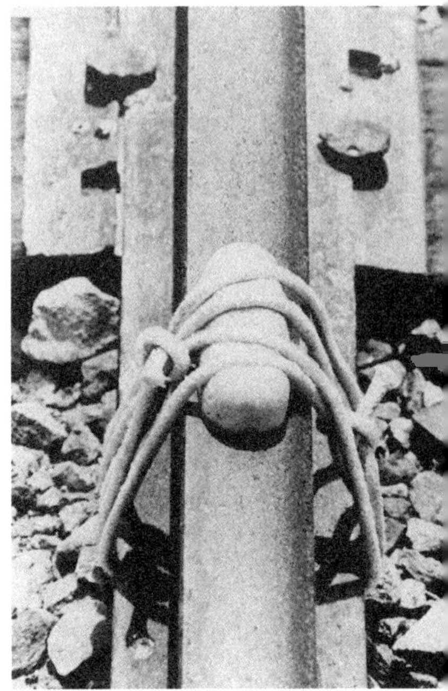

Another way of getting rid of a Twinkie!

1. Snarl, "How would you like my fist up your ass, Punk?"
2. If this turns him on, pour your beer down his front, look disgusted, and go off to the bathroom.
3. If he follows, begging for more, grab the urine cake and stuff it in his mouth.
4. If he swallows it and smiles, throw him in the urinal trough.
5. If this makes him come, get out your leather cock ring and strangle the little fucker.

When your drugs have kicked in sufficiently and the planet is suddenly lined with marshmallow fenders, it's time to go play bumper cars for the next step in Butchopoly: the disco.

DOA—Disco on Acid

There was a time—before Disco—when it was considered nelly to dance. The dance floor was filled with men wearing scarves and noisy bracelets. Butch usually leaned against the wall looking like a wallflower who might run off to the bathroom any minute to throw up.

That was before chemical welfare. Take some acid, snort a little coke, smoke some dope, and you'll find yourself in the throes of a seizure. Now just wiggle on over to the dance floor, and—presto, you're dancing. The DJ is on your side, the song will never end, and you can convulse the whole night through. You could have danced all night. There were no other choices.

There is no standard of behavior at a disco. In the grip of drug abuse, it is socially acceptable to do anything. You may throw drinks, push your friend down the stairs, or drop dead on the dance floor. Just remember, keep dancing, even when you're taking a leak, and especially when you're passing out.

By the time Butch arrives, two hours before the place closes, the dance floor is crowded. It is socially incorrect to be one of the first two hundred people dancing. This is considered eager and Butch is never in a rush.

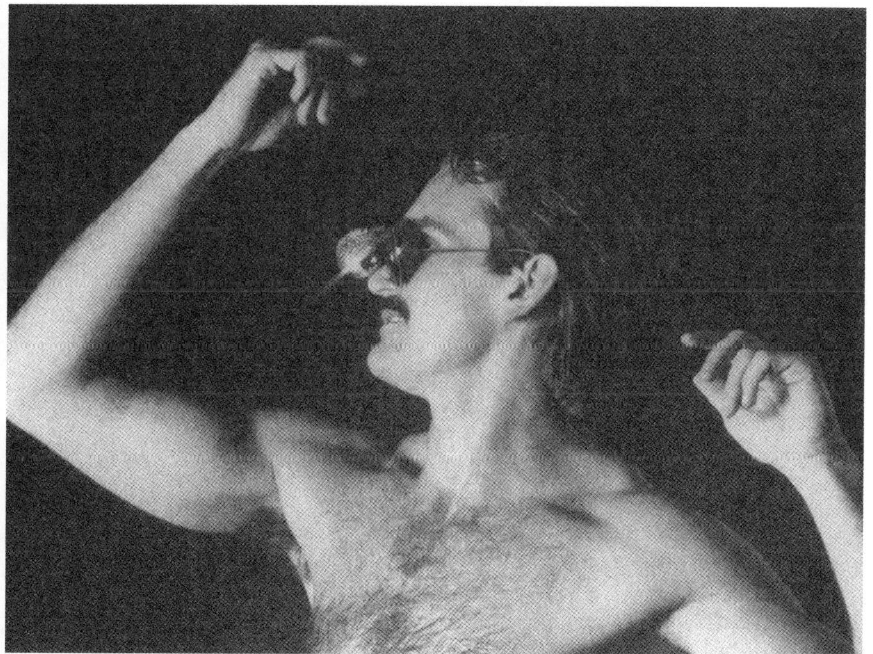

DOA—Disco On Acid

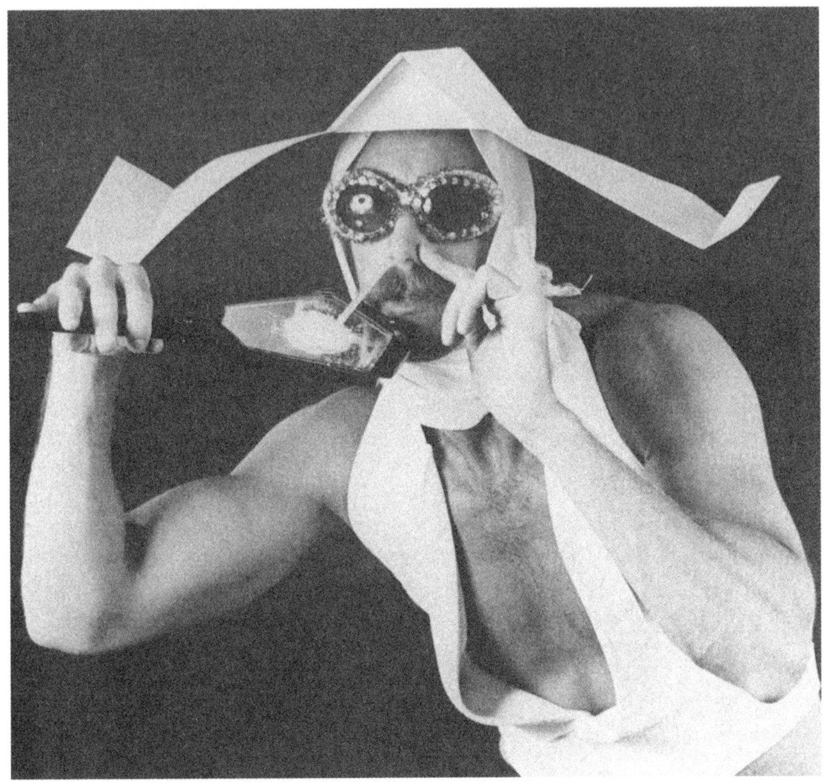

There are very few men who will admit that they want to sleep with a man dressed as a nun.

There are two areas of any respectable dance floor, the inner circle and the outer fringe. The outer fringe is less crowded. It is also less popular. The Out Crowd loves it. The Out Crowd lives to mix and match the universe. They'll mix Quaaludes and platform shoes, Dolly Parton with Twiggy, Kung Fu con Hari Kari, and Mame's entrance performed by the dancing mushrooms from *Fantasia*. Oops, someone just knocked himself out banging his tambourine on his head. Someone page Disco Nurse!

This is all very amusing, but a little too *outré* for Butch. Butch dances his way directly into the inner circle, where his gym holds court. Butch does not have a partner. Butch dances with the world. The inner circle is often so crowded there's barely room to sweat. Take a hit of poppers and let yourself go. Nod at people and smile as though you are on the best drugs that ever hit the city. Dance like this may well be the last dance on earth. These are the moments that turned the word "fabulous" into a lifestyle.

But are you dressed right? Check this list:

The Butch Disco Outfit

- 501s.
- Sweat.

Another Wild Card. Odd how it keeps popping up in Butchopoly with such tedious regularity. One might almost suspect the dealer of fraud.

The Emperor's New Drag (Butch Goes to a Pay Party)

The Pay Party Phenomenon occurs when a disco designates a particular evening as a special party and charges five times the usual admission. The disco declares a theme: "The 87th White Party!" and then orders several truckloads of pineapple for the buffet. For the extra money, the clientele gets to arrive wearing a white costume, gets to locate and ingest five times the usual quantity of drugs, and gets to use the word "party" as a verb.

No one buys tickets in advance. Conversation overheard in the locker room tends to sound like this: "If I ever go to another White Party it will be too soon." Over the urinal in the bar, like this: "Can you imagine eating thirty dollars worth of pineapple?" The party producers get nervous. "Maybe eighty-six White Parties were enough? Maybe we should have had another Black Party?"

The day of the party arrives. No tickets have been sold. Truckloads of confused pineapple flounder next to the disco floor. But wait... the boys promenading by the waves are discussing upcoming parties. Casually, someone asks if anyone is going to the White Party. Everyone holds his breath. Someone admits that he has a houseguest who has never been to a White Party and wants to go. He implores his friends to attend and provide moral stamina. Everyone immediately agrees and begins to discuss what they'll wear. The word spreads like wildfire across the beach. In hours, it ricochets through every gym in town. By dusk, the event is sold out. Telephone lines melt down as people attempt to locate enough drugs for the evening.

That night the bars are empty. Embarrassed individuals back out of bars and race to the disco, where they embarrassingly pay extra for a ticket, if they can still find one. It's a small price to pay for not being in-the-know.

Butch, of course, does not ever pay for a ticket because he knows someone, usually the party producers. He has also balled with the doorman, the ticket taker, the armed guard, the bartenders, the bottle boys, and the coat-check person.

The disco looks as on any other evening except that white lights blast the dancers every minute or so. This makes the white tutus, the white nun hats, and white go-go boots even whiter. Note that while a nun may be *amusant* on the dance floor, only a few people will want to be so amused in bed. Butch will not wear white, or at least not after he enters and takes off his shirt. He will wear 50ls and a sweaty chest.

The gossip the next day will vary. If you're talking to someone who couldn't get in the door, tell them it was the hottest party on earth. If the person you're talking to also attended, tell them the DJ was on the wrong drugs, and the last Hot White Party was number two. If you missed the party and you're listening to someone else rave, interrupt them and remind them that disco is dead.

The Funhouse (Butch at the Baths)

As Butch's drugs begin to wear off at the disco, he will either drop dead on the dance floor or he will put himself on automatic pilot and tilt in the direction of his bed. Halfway home, he may decide to go to the baths to see if he's horny.

The entrance to the bathhouse will be crammed with people desiring the answer to the same question. It is socially incorrect to talk while standing in line; this destroys the fantasy potential once inside. Lean against the wall, smoke cigarettes, and examine the pattern on the flannel shirt in front of you.

Getting into a bathhouse without the correct ID can be difficult, not to mention embarrassing. It's a good idea to bring along the doctor who delivered you to prove that you were indeed born. Butch rapidly balls with everyone who works at the bathhouse so he can get in for free.

The locker-room has the potential for locker-room fantasies, but you hardly ever see people fucking against the lockers. Maybe these people are chasing one another around the YMCA. The locker room is where people somberly choose their roving ensemble and snort their last-minute drugs.

At first it appears that the Funhouse is an informal maze of entertainment rooms, steam rooms, saunas, pools, and orgy rooms, where people flow around on invisible tracks. The Haunted House is the scariest, with lots of clanking chains and creaking leather. Adventurers on the Jungle Ride explore the darkest recesses of the steam room. The Pirates are raping and pillaging the orgy room. The Trolls are whistling while they work in the caverns of the maze. And when the lines to all the other rides are too long, there's usually no waiting at the pool, and on the Submarine Ride you always run into lots of festive marine life.

Butch's favorite ride is the Train. This ride slowly circles the Funhouse so he can see how all the other rides are doing. This is also known as the Window Shopper's Express. Butch is the engineer and the train immediately fills behind him. The Train proceeds around the halls until Butch stops to peer into a room. Each room has a man lying on his stomach and chain-smoking. Underneath his pillow is his popper collection, a variety of lubricants, and a pocket calculator so he can keep track of the evening's encounters. When he notices Butch's crotch, his butt begins to twitch like a cat swishing its tail or perhaps like a cobra getting ready to strike. Unfortunately, Butch has not informed the Train of the slowdown, and the Train telescopes into Butch. Annoyed, Butch moves on.

There are several busy intersections in the Funhouse where Butches congregate for a little friendly Posing. Butch stops to discuss the weather, why the bathhouse is having a Troll convention, and which glory holes are hot. Butch's Train again telescopes into him and, annoyed, he moves on. He tries to shake his ride in the maze, where people have gotten lost for weeks, not necessarily complaining about it, either. Butch can do the maze blindfolded, which is redundant, and quickly pivots through the crooks and crannies, leaving his riders to grope one another in search of Butch.

Butch pops out the other end of the maze, puts on his clothing, and leaves. He may or may not have come somewhere along the way, which he may or may not remember.

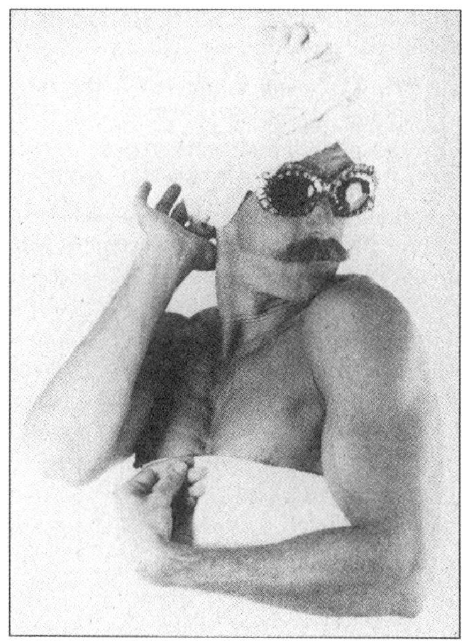

***Never* wear more than one towel at any one time.**

More important is what he was wearing.

The Butch Bathhouse Outfit

1. One white towel. This should be folded so that it hangs one millimeter lower than the end of your dick. Your towel should never hang below your knees, and you should never wear more than one towel.
2. Wear your keys on your left ankle.
3. Switch your sunglasses to an Ambermatic pair that will remain dark in hallways, but lighten in the darker corners so you can at least partially visualize who is out there.

There is one recurring nightmare at the Funhouse; it happens when people attempt to communicate.

A Note on Exchanging Phone Numbers

Some women find it difficult to achieve orgasm unless their partner happens to whisper, "I love you." Some gay people find it difficult to achieve orgasm without immediately exchanging phone numbers. Butch has never had this problem, but his partners sometimes do. Trick will plead for a number as though the number is somehow a seal of approval. If Butch says no, Trick may immediately become comatose or, worse, vicious. So Butch gives him a phone number; no one said it had to be *his* number. Butch makes sure it has seven digits.

A slightly stickier problem arises when Trick gives Butch his phone number. Everything will be all right until Butch is at a movie one week later. A very crowded movie. Butch will notice Trick sitting fifteen rows in front of him. Butch will scrunch down in his seat. Trick will spot him and wave. Butch'll pretend he doesn't see him. Trick will stand up and wave his arms. Butch'll lean over and pretend to tie his shoes, even though he's wearing boots. Trick will stand on his chair and scream, "Hey, Butch, how come you never called?" and everyone in the theater will turn around and stare at Butch, thinking, Yeah, Butch, how come?

Calmly Butch will look Trick in the eye and reply, "Because you were a bum lay and I lost your number."

How to Lose Phone Numbers

- Put it under someone else's windshield wiper.
- Paste it on the wall of a stall at the bus terminal restroom.
- Send it to Scientology requesting information on their free personality profile.
- Seal it in a bottle and throw it into the ocean.
- Mail it to someone starting a time capsule.
- Give it to the next person who asks for your phone number.

If Butch discovers that he is horny at the Funhouse and window shopping is becoming tedious, he will take the next step in Butchopoly.

The Levis Conquests (Or Butch at the Glory Holes)

The Glory Holes are where Butch gets off. Anonymous fantasies reign there in all their glory. In the shadows of sleaze, Science Fiction fucks Great

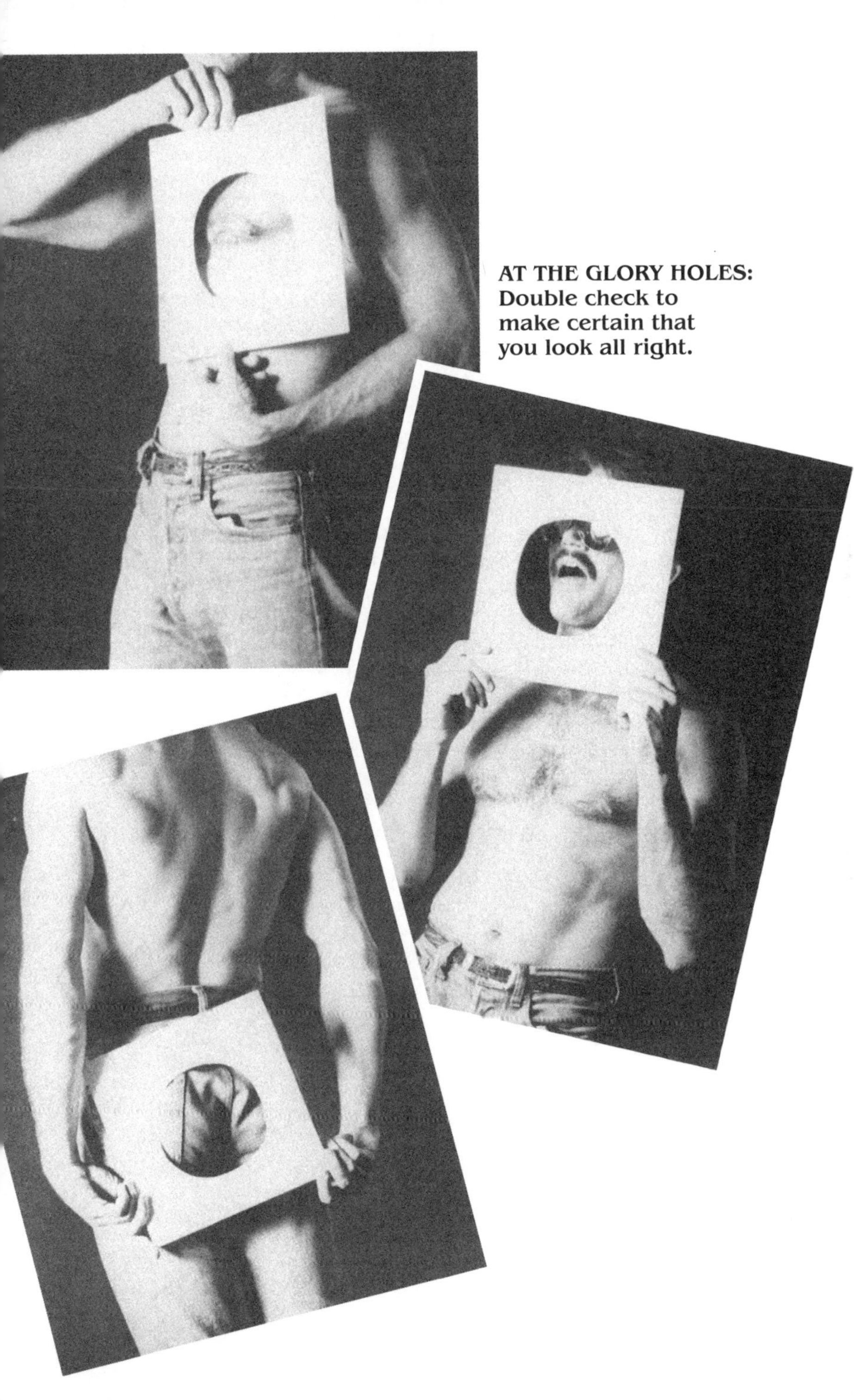

AT THE GLORY HOLES: Double check to make certain that you look all right.

Moments in History. If it happened, utilized hot uniforms or bizarre metal contraptions, and can be transferred to some kind of toilet, the men at the Glory Holes will restage it.

There are two kinds of sex to be relished at Glory Holes: macrosex and microsex. Both are a hit with Butch because neither involve one-on-one sex, which oftentimes results in embarrassing after-sex conversations or the dreaded phone number exchange. Glory Holes are popular because they are devoid of unpleasant reminders of reality. Talking is socially incorrect in the shadows unless the talk is dirty or involves the exchange of drugs. Otherwise, there is nothing that could be said that wouldn't be more impressive acted out. Field trips from the School for the Deaf always pick up interesting new signing techniques at the Glory Holes.

Macrosex occurs in the larger rooms. This is where a group of people connect as many erogenous zones as possible. A swarm of hands and mouths tweak, suck, pinch, lick, slap, bite, poke, chew, and tickle anything that will respond to stimulation. It's as though you're cruising through a sexual car wash and all genitalia are duly scrubbed. Naturally, afterward, there's no

What Butch Will Wear at the Glory Holes and Why

Butch will wear 501s, sunglasses, and one of the following accoutrements, depending on his whim.

ITEM	FANTASY
Armband	Crabbe in *Flash Gordon*
Leather cord	Quinn in *Viva Zapata!*
Harness	Reeves in *Hercules*
Construction hat	Cooper in *The Fountainhead*
Red suspenders	McQueen in *The Towering Inferno*
Open workshirt	Newman in *Cool Hand Luke*
Neckerchief	Eastwood in *The Good, the Bad, and the Ugly*
Military hat	Holden in *The Bridge on the River Kwai*
Leather gloves	Brando in *The Wild Ones*
Down vest	Reynolds in *Deliverance*
Tuxedo bow tie	Connery in *Goldfinger*
An incredible tan	Adam looking for another Adam

annoying conversation, because who can you talk to? You didn't ball with a whom, but with a what. Say you just got done by a hunky octopus wearing drag from The History of the Uniform. Simply tweak one of his suction cups in gratitude and move on.

Microsex occurs with one part of a person. It generally takes place in one of the smaller cubicles, no larger than closets. The walls between have little holes and it is possible to reach into other people's closets or to poke various parts of your body at them. Remember the Halloween Carnival in the third grade? There was a cardboard box labeled "Brains" with a hole inside. When you reached in your hand went into a bowl of spaghetti. Now you can fuck the spaghetti. And pretend it's fettuccine. And whoever heard of exchanging phone numbers with a plate of fettuccine?

Can an Asshole Be Butch?

Butch has a well-established reputation for being an extremely hot fucker. In the continuously erasing pages of everyone's address book, Butch still reads, loud and clear, "*****Top Man." At the Glory Holes, it's strictly "Take a number, please."

Unfortunately, being a legend in his own time may sometimes work against Butch. What can Butch do if he wants to get fucked? The best current solution is for Butch to get fucked at Glory Holes. This allows Butch to select the penis of his choice and get fucked to his heart's content without jeopardizing his reputation in a world that has forced Butch onto a pedestal with his ass way out of anyone's reach.

A minor problem may arise. Afterward, how does Butch get out of his cubicle without being seen? Easy. He climbs over a wall and emerges from a different cubicle. Unfortunately, this could become more difficult if you've taken a great many downs.

A major problem may arise. What if Butch likes getting fucked a lot? There is no immediate solution to this dilemma. However, looking at the history of Butch in perspective, we may recall that time when Butch was forced to stand on the sidelines of the dance floor watching the queens have all the fun. When drugs arrived, it became socially acceptable for Butch to cut up on the dance floor. Who knows?

The last step in Butchopoly is the most dangerous Wild Card of all. This card may appear at any moment. The hazard in this card is that Butch may find himself ensconced in a relationship. This would completely destroy any possibility for the aspiring Butch to attain true Butch-hood. The best tactic for countering this card is a nap.

Chez Moi (Or Butch at the Laundromat)

Butch does not like to take people home because they are often so taken with his Butch environment they refuse to leave. However, Butch is sometimes absentminded or horny and occasionally forgets this credo.

Adjacent to the gay diner in every gay neighborhood is a gay laundromat, which is where Butches like to congregate and observe one another's laundry. This is a fun time to find out who has the dirtiest towels, who is sneaking bleach with his 501s, and who has a new soap for greasy sheets.

Butch's sheets always have to go through the washer at least twice, and his towels spin the dryer into a nervous breakdown. As Butch is stuffing his damp-towel collection into his pillowcase, he will realize that the dryer has just digested his Glory Hole money. So Butch makes the Big Mistake. He takes someone home.

Immediately upon ejaculation, Trick will fall asleep. He will recite passages from *The Leatherman's Handbook* in his sleep, punctuated with animated snoring. Butch will poke Trick, to no avail. Butch will turn on the television, the Waring blender, the shower, the clock radio, and then flush the toilet. Butch wants to go out. Trick begins talking dirty in Italian. Butch is in for the evening.

Another problem occurs if Butch and Trick do handful of drugs, snort tumblers of poppers, fuck like bunnies, and then pass out. Butch will not wake up until the sun screams through the holes in the quilt over the window the next morning. Butch will then be face to face with a still snoring, tousle-haired Trick. Butch will not be amused and he'll shut his eyes and hope that Trick will awaken, quietly get up, and leave.

This never happens. Instead, Trick will awaken, stretch several dozen times in order to wake Butch up, then plant a foul-tasting kiss on Butch's mouth. Trick will leap out of bed and race into the kitchen with some misguided notion of making breakfast. One look in Butch's refrigerator should convince him that this is not the House of Eggs Benedict, and it would be wise to quietly exit.

This never happens either. If Butch can't get Trick to leave, Butch may have to get up, get dressed, and lie about having to go visit an extremely contagious friend— alone.

Tricking at home should be restricted to afternoon hours. Afterward, blow out the pilot light in the water heater and tell the trick if he doesn't leave in ten minutes he'll die. There are, of course, other ways:

How to Get a Trick to Leave

- Say, “Hey, look, a crab!”
- Take a leak and complain that it burns.
- Recommend a mouthwash to Trick.
- Recommend a few exercises to tighten up Trick’s ass.
- Recommend a psychiatrist to Trick.
- Start watching television with your headset on.
- Rip the sheets off your bed and burn them.
- Pretend that you’ve gone insane.
- Look at the clock and gasp, “Oh, my God! My two-hundred-and-forty-five-pound, muscle-bound, six-foot-six, extremely jealous lover, who happens to be a black belt in karate, is getting off work down at the police station house and will be home any second.” Sometimes, unfortunately, this will cause Trick to linger even longer.

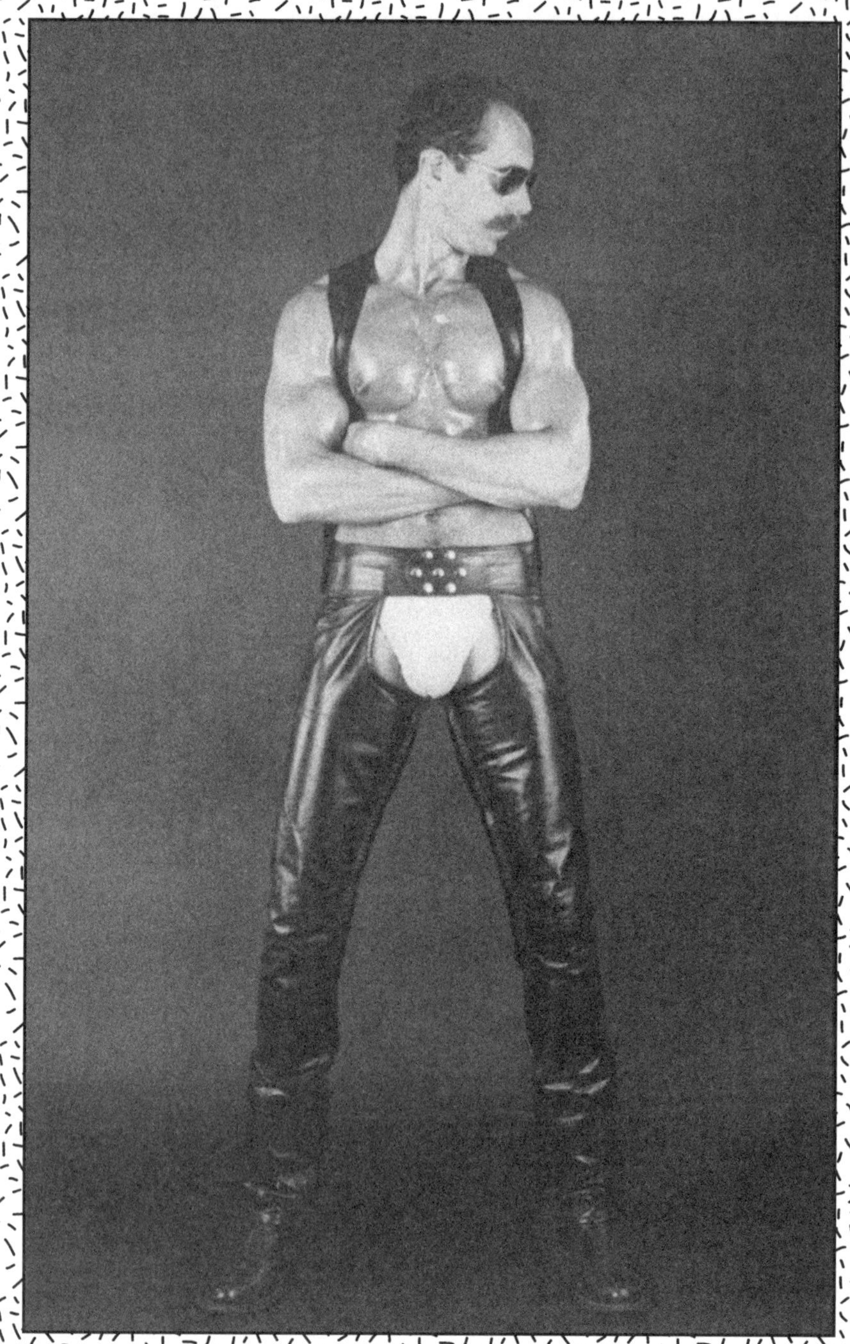

Ask Butch

(By Gertrude Stein)

Dearest Gertie,

It hardly ever happens but sometimes someone asks me home. After we're done, they always want me to leave immediately. I wonder if I'm not Butch enough. Haven't I killed all the lions in Africa? Haven't I fought every bull in Spain? Haven't I fished Idaho to death? I'm running out of things to shoot.

Your pupil,
Ernest Hemingway

Dear Ernest,

Now Ernie, stop shooting things. Concentrate on those Butch short stories with all those Butch short sentences with no adverbs, no dependent clauses, and no feelings.

Read my lips, Ernest, No Emotions.

And stop sniffling!

G.S

Dear Mme Stein,

So I drink too much, so what? And when I see other people moping around the bar, I like to go over and spread a little cheer. After all, misery loves company.

I know,
Arthur Rimbaud

Dear Arthur,

Read what another reader writes to share:

Dear Mme Stein,

I'm not moping around, I'm just spaced out. Anyone paying any attention to the latter part of the nineteenth century is spaced out. Give me my absinthe and a dark corner in the Latin Quarter and leave me alone.

Times have never been worse,
Paul Verlaine

Dear Madame Stein,

Excusez moi, *but I'll take Dijon, if you don't mind. And after lunch, I'll take Italy. If I say I'm Butch, then 1 am.* N'est-ce pas?

The Emperor

Dear Napoleon,

Are you aware that a pink, custard-filled dessert has just been named after you? And there is a plot by some dishy Paris decorators to name an entire line of furniture after you? I'd think twice about Brunch.

G.S.

My dear Miss Stein,

Doesn't jumping out of numerous jets without a parachute count for anything? How about all the rapidfire, anonymous sex I'm always having? Hey, I have no emotions. Certainly I'm a perfect candidate for the Butch Hall of Fame.

Warmly,
James Bond

Dear James,

Certainly not! You're too fond of your tuxedo and you know far too much about after-dinner drinks.

G.S.

Dear Stein,

Aaaaaaitteeeee-aiiiiieeeee-aaaie.
Aie?

Thanks, Tarzan

Dear Tarzan,

Better, but not deep enough. Keep yelling in your pillow each morning. It'll get Butcher. G.S.

P.S. You were seen running around the beach the other day in a leopard skin bikini. Have you no shame?

Dear Miss Stein,

How come I don't got no one to work out with on the weights? 'Cause I'm only three feet tall, huh? You wait. I'm gonna get real big real fast and show you guys.

Hey,
Attila

Dear Attila,

Rape and pillage, rape and pillage, is that all you short Huns ever think about?

G.S.

Dear Lady Stein,

They said I couldn't get into the glory holes because I'm too fat. I'm hardly fat at all. I'm really pissed off. Really. I may even hit someone.

I mean it,
The Marquis de Sade

Dear Marquis,

Relax, it wasn't your weight, it was the spike heels with the riding crop. Remember, *riding* boots go with riding crops.

G.S.

Dear Señorita Stein,

I just saw a fabulous movie called Where the Boys Are. *I love boys, especially nice young ones. Forget Butch, I want to be young. I hear the Fountain of Youth is right next to Ft. Lauderdale.*

Oh boy, here I come,
Ponce de León

Dear Ponce,

And when you find the Fountain of Youth, you can start treatments at Elizabeth Arden.

G.S.

Dear Mistress Stein,

Are men insane or what? They all throw my phone number away. Me, the father of the country. Not the mother, not the sister, not even the country's best girlfriend.

It's me, Daddy,
George Washington

Dear George,

They are not throwing your number away, they're spending it. Those little cards that you hand out with your picture on them also happens to be money. You overachiever!

G.S.

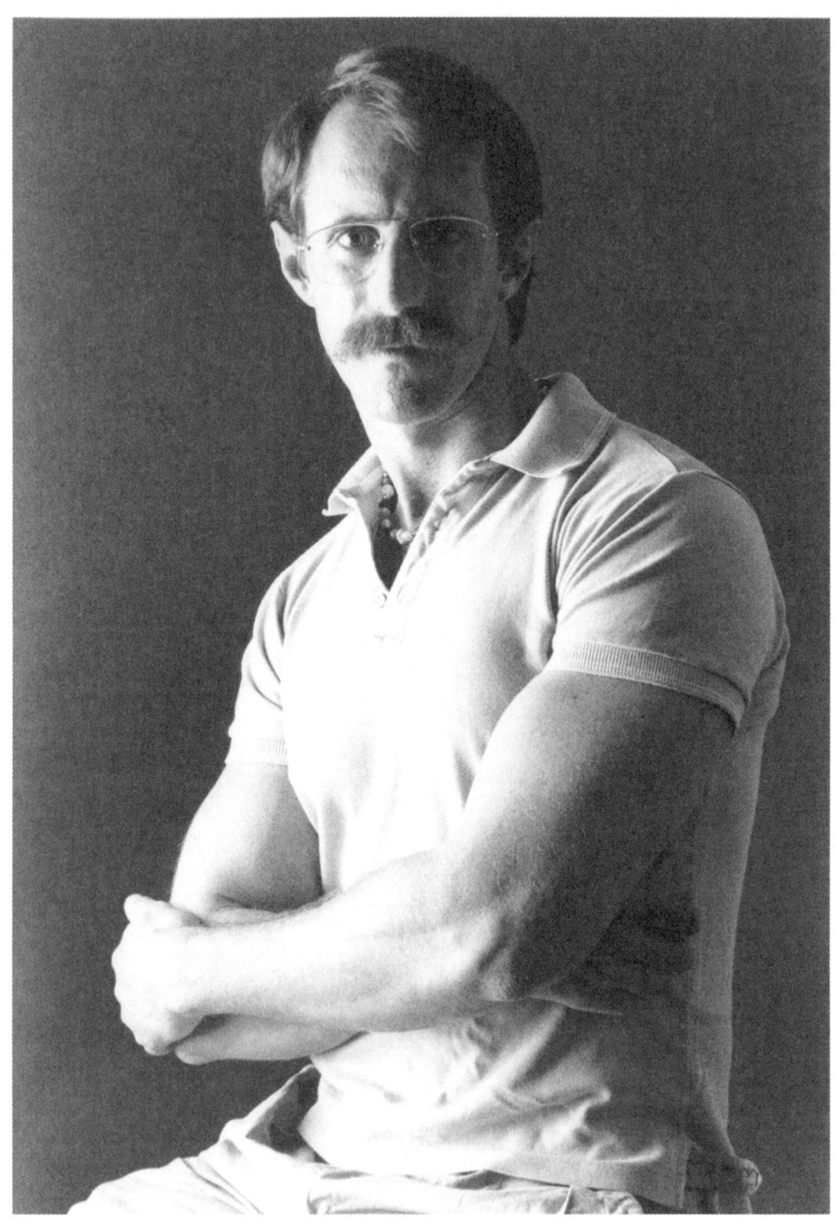

In Loving Memory of Clark Henley
May 10, 1950 – August 20,1988